Reading the Bible
in the Global Village:
Helsinki

Reading the Bible in the Global Village: Helsinki

Heikki Räisänen
Elisabeth Schüssler Fiorenza
R. S. Sugirtharajah
Krister Stendahl
James Barr

Society of Biblical Literature
Atlanta

READING THE BIBLE IN THE GLOBAL VILLAGE:
HELSINKI

Library of Congress Cataloging-in-Publication Data

Reading the Bible in the global village: Helsinki / Heikki Räisänen ...
   [et al.].
     p.   cm.
   Includes bibliographical references.
   ISBN 0-88414-019-9 (pbk)
   1. Bible—Criticism, interpretation, etc.—Congresses. I. Räisänen,
Heikki.
   BS531 .R43 2000
   220.6—dc21   •   00-37534

Krister Stendahl, "Biblical Theology, Contemporary," is reprinted from
The Interpreter's Dictionary of the Bible: An Illustrated Encyclopedia, 4 vols.
(New York and Nashville: Abingdon Press, 1962), 1:418–32. Used with
the permission of Abingdon Press.

Elisabeth Schüssler Fiorenza, "The Ethics of Biblical Interpretation: Decentering Biblical Scholarship," is reprinted from *The Journal of Biblical
Literature* 107/1 (1988): 3–17.

James Barr, "Evaluation, Commitment, and Objectivity in Biblical Theology," is adapted and reprinted from *The Concept of Biblical Theology* (London: SCM Press and Minneapolis: Fortress Press, 1999; copyright © 1999
by James Barr), 189–208. Used with the permission of the author and of
SCM Press and Augsburg Fortress.

This book is printed on recycled, acid-free paper.

00 01 02 03 04 05 06 07 08 09 — 10 9 8 7 6 5 4 3 2 1

MANUFACTURED IN THE UNITED STATES OF AMERICA

Contents

Preface

Kent Harold Richards

The Society of Biblical Literature launched an annual International Meeting outside North America in 1983. Since that time, these meetings have provided an opportunity for biblical scholars from around the world to share the results of their research, to explore emerging methods, tools, and approaches to biblical scholarship, and to exchange ideas and views with colleagues from other parts of the globe. This volume is the first in a new series to be published by the SBL under the general title "Reading the Bible in the Global Village"; the volumes in this series are intended to provide access to some of the fruits of the SBL International Meetings for those who are unable to participate in person.

This volume derives from the 1999 SBL International Meeting in Helsinki, Finland. Heikki Räisänen, Professor of New Testament Exegesis at the University of Helsinki, delivered the opening plenary address. R. S. Sugirtharajah, Senior Lecturer in Biblical Hermeneutics at the University of Birmingham, and Krister Stendahl, Andrew M. Mellon Professor of Divinity, Emeritus, at Harvard Divinity School, responded to Räisänen's address at the International Meeting, and have adapted their responses for publication here. Elisabeth Schüssler Fiorenza, Krister Stendahl Professor of New Testament and Ministerial Studies at Harvard Divinity School, was subsequently invited to contribute a written response for inclusion in this volume.

Since Räisänen's address and the responses to it make reference to and substantial use of Stendahl's article on "Biblical

Theology, Contemporary" from *The Interpreter's Dictionary of the Bible* (Abingdon Press, 1962) and Schüssler Fiorenza's 1987 SBL Presidential Address, "The Ethics of Biblical Interpretation: Decentering Biblical Scholarship," published in the *Journal of Biblical Literature* 107/1 (1988), those pieces have been reproduced in this volume as Appendix 1 and Appendix 2 respectively. At Stendahl's suggestion, Appendix 3 reproduces the chapter on "Evaluation, Commitment, and Objectivity in Biblical Theology" from the recent volume by James Barr, Distinguished Professor of Hebrew Bible, Emeritus, Vanderbilt University and Regius Professor of Hebrew, Emeritus, Oxford University, entitled *The Concept of Biblical Theology* (SCM Press and Fortress Press, 1999) The SBL gratefully acknowledges the cooperation of Abingdon Press, SCM Press, and Fortress Press in allowing materials published under their imprint to appear in this volume, and thanks James Barr for his assistance in revising the chapter from his book for its publication here.

SBL International Meetings

1983 – Salamanaca	1992 – Melbourne
1984 – Strasbourg	1993 – Münster
1985 – Amsterdam	1994 – Leuven
1986 – Jerusalem	1995 – Budapest
1987 – Heidelberg	1996 – Dublin
1988 – Sheffield	1997 – Lausanne
1989 – Copenhagen	1998 – Cracow
1990 – Vienna	1999 – Helsinki
1991 – Rome	2000 – Cape Town

Chapter 1

Biblical Critics in the Global Village

Heikki Räisänen

"Positivist Historicism" Challenged by "Liberating Praxis"?

It is commonplace knowledge that our world is becoming a "global village" which means that "the days of religious and cultural isolationism are at an end."[1] Globalization has even affected the world of biblical studies, which has undergone a "fundamental and radical shift."[2] It would seem that the wish expressed by Elisabeth Schüssler Fiorenza in her much-cited presidential address to the Society of Biblical Literature is now coming true. Twelve years ago she invited the guild of biblical scholars to accept public-political responsibility and, in doing so, to become "a significant participant in the global discourse seeking justice and well-being for all."[3] This transition would amount to a "paradigm shift" from "scientist ethos" to "a critical interpretive praxis for liberation."[4]

In the same vein, R. S. Sugirtharajah speaks for many when he stresses "the need for biblical scholars to be sensitive to the people of other faiths." Some of the biblical materials are to be "re-read" "in the light of the multi-faith context"; one has to "reformulate the message," "investing the text with new meanings and nuances."[5] He claims that the primary concern of an interpreter lies "both in transforming social inequalities" and "also in bringing racial and religious harmony among peoples of different faiths."[6] Others agree, e.g., Luise Schottroff: the goal of New Testament interpretation is "the liberation of all humankind to a life of fullness and justice"; whereas, at the same time, the claim that Jesus is the only mediator of salvation must be rejected as "Christian imperialism."[7] In this new paradigm (if indeed it is new), various feminist, liberation-theologist, postmodern, ideological-critical, and post-colonial concerns converge. For the sake of brevity, I shall call it the "liberationist approach."

There is, we are told, one great obstacle on the road to liberation, which, fortunately, is rapidly becoming obsolete,[8] and that is the old paradigm of historical-critical exegesis in the "First World." Hostile descriptions of this mighty dinosaur abound.[9] "Scientific antiquarian"[10] Western exegesis has subjected the Bible to "abstract, individualized and 'neutralized' reading,"[11] characterized by positivism, empiricism, or "radical detachment."[12] "In analogy to the natural sciences," this exegesis "sought to establish facts objectively."[13] It is said to be "nontheological and nonreligious" (though carried out by male clerics);[14] yet its methods "were used to justify the superiority of Christian texts and undermine the sacred writings of others."[15] Its "apolitical reification of the Bible as the Word of God"[16] was in effect a highly political undertaking which served colonial oppression.

> The Bible is constituted as a frozen artifact of a classical age long past, and its meaning can only be activated and re-presented by the experts in the metropolitan centers in their lineage of scholarship. Under the rubric of "objectivity" and "scientific inquiry," this orientalist reading circumscribes the range of issues that can be brought to the text and suppresses reading strategies by the so-called natives."[17]

The grip of this "tightly controlled paradigm"[18] was "close to total"[19] (despite its strong emphasis on "schools of thought," in the plural!);[20] it "had a stranglehold on critical practice,"[21] and it was "a pedagogical model of learned impartation and passive reception, highly hierarchical and authoritative in character."[22]

Though the list of vices is long, it can be summarized under one heading. In Sugirtharajah's words: the "original sin of the historical-critical method" is the notion of a division of labor "between biblical scholarship and theological enterprise"; the "hermeneutical gap" between the biblical milieu and the present day is thus a problem created by this method.[23]

If this is the case, then the chief of sinners must be Krister Stendahl who programmatically underlined this gap, by placing a great deal of emphasis on the distinction between what a text "meant" and what it "means."[24] If the liberationist account of the historical critics is correct, it should be applicable to Stendahl (if to anyone at all). Yet anyone who briefly reflects on Stendahl's life work is likely to realize that something must be wrong with this account.

Protest Against a False Dichotomy

I do not doubt that genuine experiences of liberation underlie the liberationist rhetoric. Yet it sounds like the preaching of converts who portray their own past as darkness. It reminds me, in a somewhat alarming way, of the denigration of Judaism by Christian exegetes in bygone days. Historical critics have been forced into the role of the Pharisees of Matthew 23.

I propose a counter-thesis: far from being an enemy, historical criticism at its best can, and should, be seen as an *ally* of the liberationist enterprise. Of course the historical-critical method has not always been "at its best." There has been too much emphasis on theological ideas (at the cost of their social context); the origins of the ideas have been idealized (at the cost of their effects); comparisons with other religions have often been prejudiced, and so forth. But such shortcomings are not necessarily faults of the method. They are faults of people who did not make the best use of the method. Their errors have been criticized *within the same paradigm* by others, who have pleaded for social-scientific or *wirkungsgeschichtlich* points of view, or for fair religio-historical comparison. And if authoritarian hierarchies have loomed large, this may have more to do with local academic cultures than with the method itself.

Historical-critical scholarship was never a monolith.[25] No one critic could ever have been guilty of *all* of the vices on the list. Bultmann and his school may be justly accused of "abstract" readings, but then again they have been just as adamant opponents of claims to objectivity as any liberationist interpreter.[26] The separation of historical work from its application has always been controversial *within the paradigm*; Krister Stendahl actually wrote in protest against a strong "biblical theology" movement which fused the tasks together. Both the existentialists and the "biblical theologians" have dissented with his program, though for different reasons. Those who separate what a text "meant" and what it "means" are usually *not* the same as those who use their scholarship to justify the superiority of Christian texts over others, and so on.

I still have to be persuaded by clear evidence that any important representative of the approach ever wished to model his exegesis on the natural sciences. To be sure, there has been much talk about objectivity and dispensing with presuppositions, but such statements, as everything else, must be seen in their context, which was often a confrontation with traditional doctrinal theology.[27] In the words of James Barr,[28] who comments on Stendahl's approach, "'objectively' here means: independently of whether one advocates this theology [to be studied][29] or disapproves of it." Everyone has some purpose or agenda, but "we are not speaking about perfect objectivity."[30] It is simply a question of fairness and open-mindedness over and against special pleading and propaganda.

Barr further notes: "It has often been argued that attempts at 'objective' work involved the illusion of standing outside the stream of time and producing a result wholly independent of one's own modern position. This argument is often used in order to discredit historical-critical studies. It is one of the many myths thought up by the fertile imaginations of anti-historical writers. For, of course, it is entirely untrue that the great historical critics like Harnack, or the great theorists of critical history like Troeltsch, had any such idea of themselves."[31] Actually, the historical element in "historical criticism" has been exaggerated; Barr thinks that the study of language has been more central.[32] Thus it might be wise *to put the emphasis on the "critical" rather than on the "historical."* [33]

To repeat: a historical critic—especially one who aims at relative objectivity and attempts to distinguish between reconstruction and application (or evaluation from a modern point of view)—should be seen as an ally of the liberationist enterprise. Stendahl himself long ago clarified his position as follows: "In restricting the *primary*[34] role of the biblical scholar to the descriptive task, it was my intention to *liberate* the theological enterprise from what I perceived as 'the *imperialism* of biblical scholars' in the field of theology."[35] He also made it clear that, for him, there is no method by which one can "detect 'The Meaning' (singular and timeless) of a passage, saying, or book." The descriptive task is indispensable "for theological purposes." "It guards against apologetic softenings and harmonizations"; another advantage is "its fostering great respect for the diversity within the Scriptures."[36] Thus his concern is exactly the same as that of the liberationist interpreters, though 'descriptive' is not the best of terms in this connection, for of course *imaginative reconstruction* is demanded in the historical work.[37] 'Descriptive' should simply be taken to mean that the reconstruction is not 'prescriptive' or 'normative'.

I find the goal of global relevance to be very reasonable (if it is directed to the field as a whole and not to every single scholar; those who wish to study translation technique should be free to continue to do so). But I also think that this does not render traditional biblical criticism obsolete. New developments may be seen as improvements upon the classical paradigm, but they must also be tested against old insights.

A Test Case: A Liberationist Reading of Revelation

Schüssler Fiorenza's sophisticated "liberationist reading of Revelation's rhetoric" may serve as a test case. She rejects "detached value-neutrality"; in making sense of a text, one "inevitably privileges" some elements and neglects others.[38] Schüssler Fiorenza intentionally subordinates Revelation's "depiction of cosmic destruction and holy war to its desire for justice." She chooses to privilege those features that aim at moving the audience to struggle for God's new world. A reading which stresses the outcries for revenge would lead to quite a different perception; such a reading is therefore rejected. Interpretations which attribute the destruction of the world to God are dangerous in our time (I agree!); in contrast, liberationist interpretation claims that "John does not call for the destruction of the earth."[39] According to Schüssler Fiorenza, different interpretations "must be assessed in the terms of the theoethical values and visions they engender in their sociopolitical contexts of reading."[40] This principle seems to make utility the decisive criterion, even for historical interpretation.

For Schüssler Fiorenza, Revelation's world of vision is "cosmopolitan."[41] Its ultimate goal is "the liberation of all humanity" from oppressive and destructive powers[42] (in other words, it is identical to the goal of liberationist exegesis). She believes that the salvation envisioned does not belong to Christians alone. But it is daring to suggest, among other things, that the multitude of those who stand before God, "having washed their robes in the blood of the Lamb" (Rev 7:9-17), could consist of all those, Christian or non-Christian, who have suffered violence.[43] To be sure, Schüssler Fiorenza can appeal to Rev 18:24: Rome is destroyed because "in her was found the blood of all who have been slain on the earth."[44] But it is very questionable whether the total picture of Revelation supports the contention that its "outcries for judgment and justice" (Rev 6:9, 15:4, 18:20) "rise up not only on behalf of Christians but also on behalf of the whole earth."[45] After all, Revelation uses "dwellers on the earth" throughout as a disparaging term.[46] The liberationist reading requires a very particular exegesis of a number of passages.[47]

I would have thought that the "ethics of historical reading," as set out in Schüssler Fiorenza's presidential address, would have led to a somewhat different application. The interpreter, she said, should ask "what kind of readings can do justice to the text in its historical contexts," seeking "to give the text its due by asserting its original meaning over and against later dogmatic usurpations" (and I don't see how liberationist dogmatics could be excluded here). "It makes the assimilation of the text to our own experiences and interests more difficult and thereby keeps alive the 'irritation' of the original text. . . ."[48]

In agreement with *this* insight, it would still seem to be helpful to distinguish between the historical meaning of texts, and their potential for contemporary application. Historically speaking, John may well attribute the destruction of the world to God. If so, the interpreter has to face this. The dangers of such a vision in today's world need to be exposed, and the vision has to be critically assessed. Schüssler Fiorenza does something like this regarding John's "militarist-patriarchal" God-language: that must be changed.[49] Indeed—but why not then go all the way and admit that there are other points, too, where deliberate changes are necessary, if the texts are to be applied today: for example to visions of vengeance and cosmic destruction, or to expressions of narrow-mindedness and resentment?

These features can be suppressed in responsible applications, but they should not be removed from a reconstruction of John's world of thought. It should be admitted that John's thirst for vindication took forms which we had better avoid, as we join the struggle for justice.

I think that, contrary to the cosmopolitan reading, Revelation presents an extreme version of the biblical intolerance toward "idolaters"—the "dwellers on the earth"—who make up the vast majority of humankind. Important recent studies (of which Schüssler Fiorenza is fully aware) reject the traditional view of the context of Revelation;[50] when John wrote, Christian life in Asia minor was relatively peaceful.[51] The empire was not actively persecuting Christians; some were denounced by ordinary citizens—their neighbors, the "dwellers on the earth," who had grown suspicious of the Christians' separatist and "atheist" ways.

Schüssler Fiorenza fully recognizes that John represses other views "by vilifying their advocates and by demonizing them." "Revelation's rhetoric thus shares in a potentially dangerous feature of early Christian rhetoric that cultivates a highly polemical stance towards outsiders and dissenters and thereby establishes Christian identity over against 'the other.' Interpreters reinscribe this rhetorical gesture of vituperation, silencing, and repression when they characterize John's opponents as gnostic heretics or unfaithful Jews."[52] What Schüssler Fiorenza fails to see is that similar demonizing takes place in John's attacks on the 'dwellers on the earth'; this gesture of vituperation is reaffirmed whenever their religious practice is characterized as 'idolatry' (an issue that will concern us later on in this essay).

If the strong non-dialogical, and even sectarian, side of the Bible is suppressed in exegesis, then it cannot be adequately dealt with. It is better to admit its existence, wrestle with it and criticize it openly.[53] It is our questions, not our answers, that should be affected by modern concerns.

The Case of Anti-Judaism

At one point, the shift from polemics to interfaith harmony gained ground on all sides, even within the historical paradigm. Biblical scholars have become aware that the New Testament has played a role in the sufferings of the Jews in Christendom. Gospel passages which speak of "(the) Jews" in a negative tone as opponents of Jesus have contributed to the hatred that many Christians have shown towards Jews. As a remedy, there are now new translations that are produced and old ones revised, in which the word "Jews" is not used in the exclusive sense as enemies of Jesus. It is no longer "the Jews" who seek to kill Jesus according to John 7:1, but "the leaders of the people" (*Contemporary English Version*, 1995), and so forth.

The goal of such proposals is admirable, but the means are open to serious doubt. Unfortunately the harmful (and historically incorrect) castigation of an entire people is hardly a feature that was falsely introduced to the text as an afterthought by its interpreters. It is John, himself, who uses the term "Jews" in a way that has proved disastrous. Ordinary Jews appear in a bad light simply because they do not accept John's message of Jesus as God's only Revealer.

In my view, the injustices of the past cannot be rectified by a strained exegesis or by novel translations. They must be faced by way of a frank criticism of the text itself (which might very well lead to some footnotes in our Bibles).[54] The same holds true of modern "ecumenical" portraits of Paul who, in my view, distanced himself from "normal" Judaism in such a radical way that today few Pauline scholars dare to admit it.[55]

Justice must be done to Judaism and the Jews, but not by artificial exposition. And justice should have been done to them from the start—precisely by historical critics! That it was rarely done was not a fault of the method, but of its practitioners. They were not *sufficiently* committed to a genuine historical interest, but were guided by their religious hopes (of establishing a contrast between Judaism and the message of Jesus, or of Paul). One should have been more conscious of studying a *process* for which it is necessary to step into the shoes of the different (conflicting) parties in turn. However, splendid exceptions such as George Foot Moore prove that it could have been otherwise.[56] Indeed, when the change finally occurred, it took take place within the historical paradigm, in particular due to the work of E. P. Sanders[57] (who, however, had many predecessors).[58]

The Case of Anti-Canaanaism

To return to the translation reform, in John 8:13 "the Pharisees" assert that Jesus' testimony about himself "is not true." It has been claimed that "the Pharisees" could better be rendered as "some of the people there," "since obviously not all of the Pharisees alive at that time would have addressed Jesus simultaneously in one unified chorus."[59] True enough! Yet the task of a translator must be to render the account as portrayed in the text rather than to express his or her view of what "really happened." Were we to change all passages where something "obviously" could not have happened that way, we would have to rewrite the entire Bible (and the result would be a rather slim volume).

Even if a translator wished to correct only the most obvious distortions, the task would soon prove impossible. For one thing, why should such corrections be limited to the portrayal of the Jews? What about the picture given in the Hebrew Bible of the Canaanites? Jon Levenson notes, and I am happy to quote a first-rate *Jewish* scholar here, that this picture "parallels the polemical misrepresentation of Pharisaism (or Judaism) in the New Testament."[60] Actually the New Testament polemic against Jews appears rather pale if compared to those passages in the Hebrew Bible in which the annihilation of the polytheist neighbors is required, and put into practice.

Historically, it is of course unlikely that a conquest in such a bloody manner ever took place; the biblical accounts reflect the grim fantasies of some people many centuries later. Unfortunately, Christians who read the story took it for history and, what was worse, a model to be acted on. The Puritan emigrants applied it to the "red Canaanites."[61] Not surprisingly, native Americans may feel forced to read the Exodus stories with Canaanite eyes.[62] Likewise, Palestinian Christians wrestle with the issue that the Bible appears to offer them injustice, and death to their national and political life.[63] In the interpretations of some people, they are Amalek.

Reading the Exodus story from the point of view of its Canaanite victims may be regarded as a post-colonial insight (which also corrects standard liberation theology); it represents "the impact post-colonialism should have on biblical critics and readers. They could no longer ignore either the existence of the colonized within the texts of the Bible or promote reading practices which erase their existence."[64] Reading like a Canaanite will not correct colonialism's past catastrophic intentions, but it might help the "religious academy" not to repeat them.[65] I agree; yet something like this should have been clear to the critics from the start! (Again: if it was not, then that was not a fault of the method, but of its practitioners; this is a question of studying a process, and such study entails giving a fair hearing to all parties. But it is true, as David Clines shows, page after page, that there has been far too little critique of the biblical texts; that especially after the rise of dialectical theology commentators have far too readily adopted the point of view of the text even in those cases when it is morally dubious.)[66] In any case, Marcion had already recognized that the human rights of the Canaanites were violated by Yahweh's troops.[67] In the eighteenth century, the entire critical enterprise was prompted by moral issues like this. Harnack deplored the effects of the war passages of the Old Testament in Christendom.[68] Today, Gerd Lüdemann, a modern "historicist" if there ever was one, gives a devastating moral critique of such "dark sides" of the Bible as the ban on the Canaanites.[69]

An Indian Reading of the Polemic Against Idols

I wish to make special mention of George Soares-Prabhu's Indian reading of the satire on the idols in Isaiah 44:9-20.[70] This astute article likewise points out matters which should have been recognized by any critical reader of the text; they become crystal clear when put into a "post-colonial" context by someone intimately involved.

The text is very offensive to Indian spirituality, for which 'idol worship' is a normal and edifying religious practice and the worshiped 'idols' are "recognized as visual theologies of great depth and power."[71] Of course, even the simplest worshiper in India does not worship wood and stone. The text must be recognized to be "a damaging and therefore sinful misrepresentation of a people's religion and culture."[72] The biblical author's exclusivism is not surprising, given his situation. His people in exile had lost all confidence in their history, and this feeling is the "seedbed of extremist nationalism and religious fundamentalism."[73] "If the nations are to be saved, it can only be by abandoning their history and accepting the history of Israel as theirs… This summons to alienation, only too familiar to the victims of the colonial Christian mission, is hardly a message of hope. . . ."[74]

Soares-Prabhu concludes that in the Hebrew Bible there is a "distinct anti-gentile bias" that in some ways parallels the anti-Jewish bias in Matthew and John, which "also emerged from a situation of a desperate struggle for self-definition." The anti-gentile bias has been "no less catastrophic in human history" than has the anti-Judaism of the New Testament; it has resulted "in a destruction of peoples and cultures even more devastating than the Holocaust." Soares-Prabhu notes that the "massive destruction" of temples and "cherished religious texts" in South America and in Asia (including India) "was the work not of the 'barbarous' conquistadores . . . but of the pious friars accompanying them, fired with zeal for the only god of the Bible and a paranoid hatred of 'idolatry'. The history of Christianity has been extraordinarily destructive of peoples and cultures, and this is surely at least partly because of the fanatical iconoclasm of the Bible, which is the dark side of monotheism." Thus, "'pluralist' Indian readings of the Bible" can take their place beside the Jewish critique of the anti-Judaism[75] of the New Testament, and the feminist critique of biblical patriarchy "as one of the many ways in which a reading from another place can both defamiliarize and *liberate* the text."[76] In my view, here, "defamiliarize" corresponds to Stendahl's "what it meant" and "liberate" corresponds to his "what it might mean."

This is a welcome broadening and deepening of the (historical-) critical enterprise. These things should have been seen! Actually, most commentators did recognize that Isaiah 44 is a caricature. They could have taken their criticism farther.[77] Interfaith understanding can only be served, if the anti-dialogical sides of the Bible are recognized as such—and criticized accordingly.

Sachkritik *is Nothing New*

Historical critics have sometimes pleaded for detached objectivity, but in practice they rarely abstained from value judgments at crucial points. Their practice did not quite conform to their theory. We might even say that their practice has been more adequate than their theory. Reading the classics of the discipline one constantly encounters astute *Sachkritik*, especially criticism of fanaticism and intolerance. To be sure, the opponent in view is oppressive church structures rather than global injustice (one hopes to "help to liberate the gospel from theology"[78]); a truly global vision has not yet emerged. For instance, at the turn of the century, Paul Wernle deplored the way in which the Fourth Gospel depicted Jesus as "the author of exclusiveness and fanaticism of faith," and Heinrich Julius Holtzmann recognized a "murderous messianism" in the book of Revelation.[79] This kind of criticism receded into the background with the rise of dialectical theology; once again it should be taken up and developed in the direction of a full-blown moral evaluation of the Bible and its effects, now in the global context.[80]

Moreover, it could (and should!) have been part of the task from the beginning to engage the "effective history" as well. Stendahl tells of being asked why he had, in his writing, been so preoccupied with "two topics: Jews and women." His answer, in retrospect, was this:

> The Christian Scriptures contain stuff that has proven calamitous to both Jews and women. The nonapologetic thrust of descriptive biblical theology allows us to face that problem squarely. It suggests a hermeneutic suited for the 'public health' task of theology, that is, a hermeneutic of suspicion, by which the nondesirable side effects, or even effects, of the biblical material can be discerned and counteracted. But such a task requires the honesty of not 'prettying up' the original."[81]

Why should any liberationist interpreter disagree with that?

In fact, the critical project largely started with moral criticism: with the Deist and Enlightenment wish to purify traditional religion. In Matthew Tindal's *Christianity as Old as the Creation* from 1730 an almost post-colonial touch can be discerned. Here is a sample:

> Wou'd not People, if, like the Children of Israel, they were destitute of an Habitation, be apt to think what the *Israelites*

21

did to the *Canaanites* a good Precedent; and that they might invade a neighbouring, idolatrous Nation, that never did them the least Harm; and extirpate not only Men and Women, but even their innocent Infants, in order to get possession of their Country? And I question, whether the *Spaniards* wou'd have murder'd so many Millions in the *Indies*, had they not thought they might have us'd them like *Canaanites*.[82]

It was the perception of moral problems and theological differences in the Bible that generated biblical criticism, rather than an imitation of 'secular' history, not to speak of an imitation of the natural sciences.[83] Along the way, historical criticism entered the stage and, in a sense, helped to mitigate the moral dilemma by seeing the suspect features—even the theology of the ban—as stages in a process of development within which they could be understood (without thereby being made acceptable today). Biblical critics became historical critics for the simple contextual reason that Christian tradition had always been history-oriented, and it was this that kept historical issues to the foreground.[84] These need not remain in the foreground forever—but they must be *there* as part of the picture. Only if one loses all interest in historical questions can one dispense with historical criticism (though not with a critical approach); if one does ask historical questions, historical methods become unavoidable. It does *not* follow, however, that they should be regarded as the only respectable methods (and they never were). Historical criticism is *one* useful method among several; but even if you choose not to use it (since you are interested in other questions) you can only disregard its insights at your peril.

Rather than perceiving a radical shift, I would stress the continuity of the liberationist approach with the classical critical paradigm, of which historical criticism should be seen as a part. It is possible to include new insights—from feminism, reader-response criticism, liberation theology, social anthropology, and now post-colonial criticism. Literary criticism can also be accommodated, unless it makes totalitarian claims. If it pays attention to the ideological aspects of texts, it cannot avoid coming close to and making some use of the classical approach.

Here the three-world model of Kari Syreeni is very helpful: an interpreter should pay attention both to the text world proper, and the symbolic world of the author, as well as to the real world in which he or she lived.[85]

A Personal Testimony

Am I being too apologetic? Well, of course I too am "speaking from a place," from a social location, and perhaps you allow me to insert a personal word. Whatever little I understand about dialogue, encounter, diversity and pluralism, I have learnt in critical historical work.[86] It taught me to recognize the diversity of the Bible, even of the New Testament, and to appreciate the mighty human processes involved—a rough course in self-criticism. Subsequently, it was the reading of the Qur'an with an analogous redaction-critical approach that helped me to appreciate that alien scripture. Redaction criticism is often looked down upon as old-fashioned, but of course it never consisted of the separation of redaction from tradition only; redaction criticism taught me to view the Qur'an as a theological whole rather than to just trace its components to this or that source (which was then fashionable in critical studies of the Qur'an). [87]And it was my old-style exegetical training that helped me to see the lack of fairness in many current comparisons of the Bible with the Qur'an—Allah being depicted as a cruel and capricious oriental (*sic!*) despot, while Yahweh was described positively as a numinous majesty.[88] From here it was only a short step to the recognition that justice was not always done to Judaism (or to Paul's conservative opponents) in Pauline scholarship.[89] If I have learnt anything of scholarly fair play, I owe it all to the clear-headed Scandinavian tradition which appreciates *Religionswissenschaft*, and emphasizes keeping historical and theological interpretations apart (though it can be committed to both).[90] This tradition insists that justice be done to Jews, to Stoics, to Gnostics[91]—and now to the idolaters.

23

Moral Criticism of the Bible—By Historical Critics

Moral criticism, or the ethics of accountability, called for by Schüssler Fiorenza twelve years ago,[92] should now be part and parcel of the critical enterprise. The ethical consequences of the biblical texts and their meanings are to be evaluated. This is surely one of the most crucial tasks in the global situation we find ourselves in today.[93] And this challenge is being recognized—not only among those who are consciously engaged in post-colonial criticism or the like. To name a few examples: Ulrich Luz systematically asks about the fruits of Matthew's texts.[94] Robert Carroll discusses the Bible as a problem for Christians—"the wolf in the sheepfold"—and Gerd Lüdemann exposes the "unholy" in Holy Scripture.[95] Long ago, Robert Jewett distinguished between zealous nationalism and prophetic realism in the Bible, and traced the influence of both on American history and contemporary politics.[96] More recently, Michel Desjardins has discussed peace and violence in the New Testament, likewise finding both.[97] Michael Prior has examined biblical texts about the land and their use in colonialist enterprises, including Zionism and the state of Israel.[98] He invites the guild to subject biblical traditions to an ethical evaluation which derives from general ethical principles.[99]

Luz makes a gigantic effort to follow through the effective history of the gospel of Matthew (though still largely limited to a church perspective). Even sacred texts are to be evaluated according to their fruits.[100] Even though Luz himself criticizes the historical-critical method on various points, he admits that it is precisely this method that makes it possible for the non-Christian to also "enter into a dialogue with the texts." Christian interpreters have used "God" or "Jesus Christ" as "an instrument to absolutize their own human standpoint"; "Christianity desperately needs the *ideological-critical potential of historical criticism.*"[101] In his own European context, Luz hopes to "help liberate Christians from premature pronouncements derived from the Bible about life, society, and church," by showing that the Bible cannot function "as a norm or as direct legitimator,

24

but as a source of direction, ideas, and experiences."[102] "The study of history, while prohibiting us from taking historical truths as absolute, opens the possibility of using historical truths as models or examples."[103]

Jewett distinguishes between the very different traditions of zealous nationalism and prophetic realism within the Bible. He notes that the revived zealous ideology of Deuteronomy blunted Prophetic realism, "producing massive illusions which could lead only to disaster."[104] The trajectory of Zealous Nationalism culminates in the Book of Revelation which looks forward to "the violent destruction of the entire world so that the peace of the saints could be secured."[105] "*The application of the critical methods of modern biblical scholarship allows a kind of ideology-criticism* that separates the healthy from the unhealthy components of a broad cultural legacy." At present, the decisive need for Americans is to rely upon the healthy side of their tradition, "to hold our tendencies in check."[106] Jewett hopes to contribute to this end by "recovering some of the humane and realistic components of the Biblical tradition" and by criticizing others. A critical distinction within the Bible leads to an examination of some historical effects of the different biblical ideologies, coupled with an ethical critique—a fruitful combination of what certain texts "meant" (at different times!) and what they might come to "mean" today.

A Plea for Cooperation

The proponent of a division of labor, or a distinction between operations, should be recognized as a friend, rather than enemy, of contextual theology. The proper use of historical methods can be extremely helpful, it can liberate one to do theology in a creative way. Ideological and moral criticism can—indeed must!—be accommodated within the model. This is a broadening—or making explicit—of something that has been there all along.

Theology is always contextual, and theologians must make

their own decisions. Moral criteria—from outside the studied texts—must be applied. As Mary Ann Tolbert puts it:

> To call for an ethics of interpretation is to recognize the power of the Bible in the public and private lives of people around the world today and to acknowledge both the good and evil that power has done and continues to do. I do not believe that such ethics can be derived from the Bible alone. . . . Thus, drawing on the best that theology, moral discourse, philosophical thought, science, and history can provide," Christians must "develop sets of criteria for evaluating biblical interpretations in each situation."[107]

Post-colonialism is a most justified concern. But in general post-colonial interpreters seem to realize that, while the Bible may be part of the solution, it certainly is also part of the problem.[108] A distinction between exegesis and hermeneutics, or reconstruction and application, seems implied. And I continue to insist: a colonial attitude is *not* inherent in the historical approach itself![109]

A critical attitude to the biblical record is demanded at the level of application, if one engages in earnest inter-faith dialogue. We have to opt for some trends in the Bible against others; sometimes we have to opt, say, for justice and love against the entire biblical tradition. It is only on some such basis that credible theologies can be built today. In this work, historical-critical exegesis could be an ally, insofar as the expectations are realistic. By definition, exegetical scholarship cannot liberate the world any more than can church history. Instead, the texts can be used by way of reinterpretation in the service of liberating processes (alas, they can be used for very different purposes, too).

It is underscored by liberation theologians that "life takes first place"; the "experience of life" is the "primary text."[110] This comes quite close to my own vision of the formation of the early Christian world of thought in a process in which traditions were interpreted in the light of new experiences time and again, mostly social experiences, and vice versa: experiences were interpreted in light of traditions.[111] If this is an aspect of "what it meant," it is a logical continuation of the process, when theologians (and others) engage in conscious reinterpretations of their traditions in light of their own context and present experience.[112] The contribution of historical study to theology may well consist of suggesting this model of theology as a process of ongoing reinterpretation. This could be "what it means" today.

An exegete may serve in the global village, for example, by analyzing ancient encounters (peaceful and other) of different traditions and visions, and their effects; thereby trying to do justice to all sides. In this process, traditions and figures that have perhaps been marginal in their time may become of focal interest (the book of Jonah against exclusivism; the Gentile woman who teaches Jesus a lesson against Christological imperialism).[113] Another possibility would be, in the spirit of fair play, to study the reception of the Bible by outsiders.[114] Looking at the Bible through foreign eyes may help us see some sides of our tradition in a new light. Finally, reading against the grain may prove illuminating; taking note of tensions and contradictions in the texts may make us aware of problems, reflection on which may in turn guide us toward fresh approaches in our situations.[115]

A critical approach to one's own tradition—and this alone— may give the critic the right to suggest that historical and moral criticism might be applied to other scriptures and sacred traditions as well, though the task should best be carried out by adherents of that tradition themselves. I am thinking first of all of the Qur'an and of the *sharia*, both of which can (though they need not) function as oppressive forces.[116]

There *has* been a shift, and in many ways it is to be welcomed. I think, however, that the radicalness of this shift has been exaggerated. The liberationist enterprise might profit from regarding the historical-critical paradigm, in particular that version which distinguishes between reconstruction and application, as a blessing, rather than as the original sin. Accordingly, I have been delighted in reading some recent articles by Sugirtharajah (and his thoughts could be paralleled in the writings of many other liberationists[117]). He writes:

> The interpretative task, then, requires that we read from our social and cultural locations, and interrogate the texts with our different historical questions, exploring insights about *what the texts might have meant* [!] historically and *what they mean today.*[118]

With regard to the problems of Paul and company, he states:

> We must have the hermeneutical integrity to admit the difference between our context and theirs.[119] But if we listen carefully we may rediscover in their stories and struggles our own anxieties, hopes, and questions. The documents may not possess the answers, but they may encourage us in the present and excite our imagination to act creatively and to map out an open future.[120]

I could not agree more completely!

Chapter 2

Defending the Center, Trivializing the Margins[1]

Elisabeth Schüssler Fiorenza

Initially I was quite pleased finally to receive a reply to my SBL presidential address from a plenary lecturer at a major SBL event. While my address has been quoted widely in the US and internationally, I have not had much response from the center of biblical studies. Although there were many positive responses to it, they have come mostly from the margins. "Decentering biblical scholarship" has proven to be a difficult task.

Listening to the lecture my pleasant surprise turned quickly into disappointment. This was not a serious engagement of the voices from the margins but a subtle attempt by an esteemed colleague to safeguard the center which he rhetorically marked as historical criticism and to misrepresent the margins. Moreover, although there were two responses to his lecture at this event by scholars whom he had extensively quoted, neither another feminist colleague nor I had been invited to respond. It seems that the prohibition *mulier taceat in ecclesia* continues to shape academic discourse, albeit it is no longer intended.

Most perplexingly, Heikki Räisänen's rhetoric seemed well-intentioned pleading for cooperation between historical critics and what he dubbed "the liberationist approach." Yet collaboration is only possible if differences are appreciated and acknowledged. Since he denies that a paradigm shift is taking

29

place, I will first restate my argument for the paradigm shift that seeks to decenter hegemonic biblical studies. Then I will analyze the overall rhetoric of his paper. Finally I will elaborate the ethics of interpretation as constituting the ethos of such a new paradigm. For more explication and information I refer readers to my new book *Rhetoric and Ethic: The Politics of Biblical Studies*[2] which further elaborates the ethics of interpretation proposed by my SBL presidential address.

The Rhetorical-Emancipatory Paradigm Shift

It has now been more than twenty years since I first diagnosed a paradigm shift underway in biblical studies.[3] A new paradigm seems to be evolving, especially in and through the work of feminist and postcolonial biblical critics which I have named the rhetorical-ethical or rhetorical emancipatory paradigm and which Fernando Segovia has called the paradigm of critical cultural studies.[4] In order to elaborate this emerging critical evaluative paradigm, one must explore in terms of what Krister Stendahl has called the "public health department" of biblical studies not only the theoretical frameworks, methods, and strategies of biblical interpretation, but also its institutional locus and its scholarly and educational formations.

I have argued that a paradigm shift requires not only a shift in theoretical approach but also an institutional shift. In order to fashion a rhetorical "public health department," biblical studies must be refashioned in such a way that it constitutes a public-political-religious and not just an academic-religious or theological clergy discourse. Biblical studies must be decentered in such a way that the voices from the margins of the discipline who raise the issue of power, access and legitimation can participate on equal terms in fashioning a multi-voiced center that is perpetually decentering itself.

Refashioning its exegetical, historical, and hermeneutical inquiry, biblical studies must not only engage in critical readings and evaluations of biblical discourses in terms of a public, radical-democratic ethos but also fashion critical scholarly practices that can engage such an ethos. It must ask: How has this text been used and how is it used today to defy or corroborate hegemonic political systems, laws, science, medicine, or public policy? How has biblical interpretation been used and how is the bible still used either to challenge or to protect powerful interests and to engender socio-cultural, political, and religious change? How is the bible used to define public discourse and groups of people? What is the vision of society and church that is articulated in and through biblical texts? Which readings or reconstructive models become hegemonic and which are marginalized or passed over with silence?

It must also ask: Who has authority in the field and to what ends it is used? How are students socialized into becoming biblical scholars and what is the ethos of the discipline into which they are socialized? How is "truth" established and to what ends? How is scholarly authority constructed and maintained? How does it function and in whose interest is it pursued? Are the institutional tools of biblical studies—publications, conventions, peer review procedures, and educational curricula— used to marginalize certain people, to legitimate racism and other languages of hate, or to produce knowledge and public discourses that can intervene in practices of injustice and motivate people in their struggles against it?

To commit biblical studies to asking such questions, I have repeatedly argued, would engender a transformation in the self-understanding of the discipline. It would effectively change biblical studies into a rhetorical-ethical discourse that fashions connected intellectuals who can interpret the bible in and for an increasingly cosmopolitan public. Reading the bible in the global village requires that one carefully analyzes what stands in the way of such a paradigm shift rather than reducing it to a discrete approach within the hegemonic paradigm of biblical studies as my colleague does.

Although this paradigm shift has been under way for quite some time and has brought ferment or upheaval—depending on one's political perspective—to the once stable field of biblical and religious studies, it has not been able to unseat the positivist scientific, supposedly disinterested, ethos of the discipline as Räisänen's essay documents. Hence, this emerging paradigm also is not yet able to transform biblical studies in such a way that it would no longer confine the understanding of Scripture to elite male intellectuals and restrict its audience either to the academy or to clergy education. Instead, biblical studies would seek to make available to a wider public research that is ethically accountable.

Feminist scholarship has trailblazed such a rhetorical, ethico-political paradigm of biblical and religious studies. However, the pioneering contributions of feminist theory are seldom recognized in the malestream discourses deliberating the status of the discipline. Critical feminist scholarship not only encounters resistance in the academic centers of biblical and religion studies but also often receives only a token acknowledgment in the malestream discourses of the margins. "Decentering biblical scholarship" has proven to be a difficult task not least because the hegemonic institutions of biblical studies have subtly contravened it. The essay under discussion is a case in point.

The Rhetoric of Marginalization and Misstatement

As Räisänen himself acknowledges, his essay is an apologetic discourse in defense of the centrality of historical criticism. This apologetic pathos leads him to mistake my argument for a theoretical and institutional paradigm shift and the decentering of biblical scholarship, as a rejection of historical criticism. It is more than surprising to find myself classed among the enemies of historical-critical scholarship although my work is squarely located within historical-rhetorical studies. Such a category mistake might have been avoided if he had consulted the whole body of my work.

It is odd that Räisänen does not consult my scholarly work on Revelation[5] or my feminist work[6] for clarifying his understanding of the issues. He only refers to my presidential address and my commentary on Revelation written for a general public, although in both I clearly argue from a historical-critical feminist standpoint. His misreading of my work becomes understandable when one recognizes the apologetic character of Räisänen's discourse, that seeks to defend the centrality of historical-criticism in biblical studies and attributes central status to it. Attribution of status is a characteristic of argument about discourse. Argument about status activates a pattern of thinking that marks symbols, ideas, or practices "according to their centrality or marginality to the society of the thinker."[7]

In light of my call for a decentering of biblical scholarship, Räisänen's defense of historical criticism[8] indicates that historical criticism is for him the unquestioned center of biblical scholarship. He claims that "historical critics have been denigrated [*sic*] and forced into the role of the pharisees in Mt 23" by their liberationist critics, although my address argued not for the shift from a historical to a liberationist paradigm but for a shift from a literary-cultural to a rhetorical-emancipatory or ethical paradigm of biblical studies. As I pointed out, the decentering of historical-critical studies was diagnosed quite some time ago by Frank Porter who already in 1908 spoke of historical science being replaced by a third stage of literary-cultural criticism.

Why then is Räisänen's argument not with literary-postmodern critics and exegetes who deny the referential character of language and thereby argue for the obsolescence of historical critical studies on epistemological grounds? Why does he target liberationists, who have a keen interest in history and heritage. Is it because he subscribes to the prejudice that "liberationist" interpretation is a dogmatic usurpation of the historical text in its original context and that it is not scientific but smacks of "special pleading" and propaganda? Instead of taking on postmodern literary-cultural studies he prefers to construct as his "opponent" the work of those advocating a critical rhetorical-ethical/emancipatory paradigm. If, however, Räisänen is serious in his advocacy of moral criticism one would have expected that he would join ranks with those whose epistemological framework not only allows for historical-critical reading and ethical assessment but requires it.

Hence, Räisänen's marginalization and trivilialization of what he terms "liberationist approaches" must be analyzed in rhetorical terms. What is the rhetorical problem he seeks to address and what are the interests and pathos of his arguments? What compels him to resort to such strategies of marginalization and trivialization that result in (1) homogenization, (2) co-optation, (3) misrecognition, and (4) misrepresentation?

(1) The rhetorical strategy of *homogenization* treats all others as the same and thereby overlooks their significant differences. This strategy is apparent in the beginning of his paper, where Räisänen constructs the discourse of the "liberationist approach" by quoting snippets out of context. Rather than recognizing and analyzing the differences in the theoretical proposals of Sugirtharajah, Segovia, and myself, whom he seems to consider as major representatives of the "liberationist approach," he constructs our presumed common *Feindbild* not only by citing out of context but also by not recognizing that we argue on different grounds and adopt different argumentative strategies. To quote him:

> There is we are told, one great obstacle on the road to liberation which fortunately, is rapidly becoming obsolete, and that is the old paradigm of historical-critical exegesis in the "First World." Hostile descriptions of this mighty dinosaur abound.[9]

Yet his reference to my own work does not cite a statement where I indict historical criticism tout court but refers instead to my characterization of "scientific antiquarian" scholarship. Any careful analysis of the context of this statement could have shown that I am not so much concerned with a particular method of inquiry—i.e. historical criticism—but with a scholarly ethos or mindset. I am sure that my colleagues could point to similar misreadings of their work. What is at stake here is not historical criticism as such but its central status and antiquarian mindset. The strategy of homogenizing our diverse work allows him to disregard its nuances and to sustain the hegemony of historical criticism as the center of biblical studies.

(2) The rhetorical strategy of *co-optation* defines the propos-

als and the interests of the margins as those of the master thereby functionalizing them to achieve the master's own interests. To quote Räisänen again:

> Moral criticism or the ethics of accountability called for by Schüssler Fiorenza twelve years ago should now be part and parcel of the critical enterprise. The ethical consequences of the biblical texts and their meanings are to be evaluated. This is surely one of the most crucial tasks in the global situation we find ourselves in today.[10]

This apparent agreement, however, is weakened and belied through repeated statements such as: historical criticism is to be seen as engaging the "liberationist enterprise;" shortcomings of historical criticism are shortcomings of practitioners, not of the method; the ethics of interpretation is nothing new because *Sachkritik* has always been an integral part of historical criticism, and so on. His rhetoric makes a show of being fair, reasonable, and open while at the same time deprecating liberationist work.

In short, Räisänen does everything to show that a paradigm shift has not only not taken place but that it is also not necessary:

> Rather than perceiving a radical shift, I would stress the continuity of the liberationist approach with the classical critical paradigm, of which historical criticism has to be seen as a part. It is possible to include new insights—from feminism, reader response criticism, liberation theology, social anthropology, and now postcolonialism. Literary criticism can also be accommodated, unless it makes totalitarian claims.[11]

This statement makes it clear that the center not only seeks to incorporate and swallow up approaches different from its own but also that it does so by setting the terms under which they can be accommodated. In short, what is at stake is not method but authority. What appears to be a battle of methodological "approaches" is in reality a battle for power.

(3) This strategy of co-opting and incorporating the alleged "others" of historical criticism, however, can only be main-

tained if it is combined with one of *misrecognition*. In order to maintain the hegemony of the center of power *the strategy of co-optation and incorporation* argues for the centrality of the other as the same in the constitution of self-identity. It can only do so, however, if it conceals the difference of the other in its discourses about the other by engaging in a misrecognition and misinterpretation of such differences.

For instance, at no place does Räisänen elaborate or even mention my main thesis: that a decentering of hegemonic biblical scholarship has to take place so that practitioners from different social locations can move into and reconstitute the center of biblical studies. Just as my middle-class students often do, he confuses social location with personal testimony. Rather than reflecting on the different social locations of the so-called liberationist approaches as well as his own within the traditions and institutions of biblical studies, he resorts to personal testimony for the utility of historical criticism in general and redaction criticism in particular to the liberationist enterprise.

The same misrecognition takes place with regard to my reformulation of the dualistic "meant-means" or "exegesis-application" hermeneutical pattern. Since the linguistic and hermeneutical intellectual turns have made it impossible for exegetes to say with certainty "what the text meant" or to divide the interpretive process into description and application, I suggested its reformulation in terms of an ethics of interpretation consisting of an ethics of reading that can do justice to the possible meanings of texts *and* an ethics of accountability that can articulate and make visible the power relations inscribed in biblical texts and their interpretations. Such an ethics of interpretation calls for much more than what traditionally has been understood by *Sachkritik*, although as I have stressed over and over again, it seeks to revive *Sachkritik* in biblical studies.

In addition, Räisänen repeatedly asserts that the method of historical criticism should not be blamed for having had bad practitioners. Yet this assertion conceals the major point of difference between us. It is precisely this sharp differentiation between method and practitioners that has been called into question by rhetorical criticism, hermeneutics, ideology criticism and liberation theologies. Rhetorical criticism has shown that discourses are socially constructed and speak to particular situations, hermeneutics has insisted that no understanding is possible without pre-understandings, ideology criticism asserts that all knowledge is interested, and liberation theologians have contended that knowledge is power that works always for or against the oppressed. A method is not a self-contained tool of investigation. It is only as good or as bad as its practitioners are. Social-religious location, hermeneutical preunderstandings and scientific interests are part and parcel of scientific method.

(4) Finally, because of the rhetorical strategies of concealment and misrecognition hegemonic discourse has to resort to *misrepresentation*. This can be elucidated both with respect to Räisänen's discussion of my interpretation of Revelation and with respect to how he deploys Krister Stendahl rhetorically.

First, Räisänen's discussion of my interpretation of Revelation is a blatant case of such misrepresentation. Since he takes my reading of Revelation as a "test case" for his methodological contention that "new developments may be seen as improvement upon the classical paradigm, but they must also be tested against old insights,"[12] I will pay closer attention to this injunction before discussing instances of his misrepresentation of the Revelation debate.

From the context of his statement it seems that the "old insights" against which new ones must be tested is the maxim that a historical critic—especially one who aims at relative objectivity—must distinguish between reconstruction and application (or evaluation from the modern point of view).[13] Application and evaluation, however, are not the same, as Räisänen's reduction of "evaluation from a modern point of view" suggests. Rather, application according to the "old insights" has the function to "transfer" but not to evaluate descriptive exegesis of texts and their "translation" into contemporary language in order to produce meaning that addresses contemporary problems. Insofar as interpretation and reconstruction always already are constituted by contemporary concepts, models, or frameworks, Räisänen's rhetoric conceals the fact that his own characterization of the "old insights" has already subtly shifted the terms of discussion. Why this is necessary becomes obvious when one looks at his treatment of my interpretation of the book of Revelation as a "test case."

Räisänen's rhetoric here bespeaks the old polemics against liberation theology as unscientific because of its ideological interests, rather than as an example of the moral criticism allegedly already prevalent in historical-critical studies. Even though he cites the generally accepted hermeneutical maxim that texts are multivalent and interpreters inevitably privilege some elements and neglect others, he maintains that only his "revenge" interpretation is historically correct.

In order to make his point Räisänen resorts to misrepresenting and caricaturizing my position. He accuses me of "idealizing John's perspective" although he concedes that I have recognized that Revelation's polemical rhetoric is dangerous and must be assessed and evaluated. Moreover, he concedes, that I recognize that John probably belonged to a "cognitive minority" within the communities of Asia Minor and that we have other voices in the Christian Testament that advocate adaptation to the dominant ethos. Yet he concludes from this "that the majority of Asian Christians (such as the authors and addressees of the Pastorals, Luke-Acts or 1 Peter) belonged to the small privileged elite" in order to render the picture drawn by me suspect.[14]

In addition Räisänen conjectures that I *intentionally subordinate* (emphasis added) Revelation's "depiction of cosmic destruction and holy war to its desire for justice." He further implies that the "revenge-interpretation" is historically more adequate than the interpretation in terms of justice. Whereas the "revenge-interpretation" understands Revelation in terms of "holy war" and the psychoanalytic-cultural interpretive model of "ressentiment," the "justice-interpretation" reads the same text in terms of a court-model of judgment and in light of the end of the book, the vision of the New Jerusalem which is characterized as coming down to earth. It is pictured in terms of a cosmopolitan city of wellbeing in whose "light the nations will walk" and into which the kings of the earth will bring their glory" (Rev 21:22–22:5). To interpret Revelation's outcries not as outcries of revenge but as cries for justice shifts the rhetorical tenor of the book and its meaning for its first audience as well as its contemporary readers.

Rather than engaging my historical interpretation of Revelation in terms of justice, Räisänen prefers instead to present it as methodologically flawed. Since I am critical of the "revenge-interpretation" of Revelation—an interpretation that he favors—he surmises that I violate the old methodological distinction between the historical meaning of texts and their contemporary application, between what the text meant and what it means today:

> Historically speaking John may well attribute the destruction of the world to God. If so, the interpreter has to face this. The dangers of such a vision in today's world need to be exposed, and the vision has to be critically assessed.[15]

I could not agree more and have continually called for such a critical evaluation in terms of a scale of values and visions. If the revenge interpretation is more adequate to the text in its socio-historical context than the "justice" reading which I have proposed, then Revelation must be evaluated in terms of its rhetoric of revenge. However, my argument has been that the justice-reading is more adequate to the overall textual rhetoric of Revelation and hence the book should not be evaluated in terms of revenge.

How then is one to go about settling this conflict of interpretations? In the old positivist-scientific historical paradigm one needed to show that one's own reading of the text is the correct one and that alternative readings are methodologically deficient. This is exactly what Räisänen does when he suggests that I intentionally subordinate Revelation's outcry for revenge to one of justice. Yet if the difference in interpretation cannot be settled on the level of the text when one recognizes that the rhetoric of the text allows for a range of legitimate readings, it must be adjudicated on the level of hermeneutics and ethics. The evaluation of the text's world of vision needs to recognize not only the possibility but also the legitimacy of different readings which must be adjudicated—so I argue—in terms of a scale of theo-ethical values and visions of the "good life."

Although Räisänen sees moral criticism as part and parcel of the interpretive enterprise, he claims that I make "utility the decisive criterion, even for historical interpretation." That is not what I do when I ask that "different interpretations must be assessed in terms of the theo-ethical values and visions they engender." Rather than either granting that both interpretations are adequate to the text, or questioning their adequacy and therefore demanding that they must be scrutinized as to the values and visions they promote, he chooses to put down as "utilitarian" my proposal that one must critically assess the values and visions promoted by differing interpretations. But since when is a rhetoric of values and visions "utilitarian" and not ethical-religious? Rather than simply applying the interpretation of a text to the contemporary situation one needs to spell out the criteria of evaluation and use them to assess the text and its diverse interpretations.

Anyone familiar with scholarship on Revelation will have recognized immediately that this conflict in the interpretation of Revelation is not new but has a long tradition. It is not only engendered by the multivalent symbolic language of the text but also by different traditions of interpretation rooted in different social locations. Whereas the revenge-interpretation continues the negative evaluation of Revelation in the tradition of the Reformation, especially in the Lutheran form, the justice interpretation shares in the centuries old interpretive tradition of marginal groups and social movements struggling for justice and well-being. These differences in interpretation, I have argued, can no longer be settled on the level of text or historical "facts" but must be adjudicated on the level of hermeneutical and reconstructive models of historical-religious interpretation. They can not be settled by retreating to the methodological dualism between historical exegesis and contemporary application nor by revalorizing the slogan "what the text meant" and "what it means today."

Second, it is important to see how the invocation of Krister Stendahl functions in Räisänen's argument to promote misrecognition by misrepresenting both our positions. In my reading, Stendahl is the patent victim of such misrepresentation not because Räisänen misconstrues his position but because he uses him as a central figure in the discursive chess-game of his apologia for historical criticism that supposedly leads the "liberationist approach" "ad absurdum."

Räisänen's argument circles around the dualistic slogan separating "what the text meant" from "what it means" today,[16] which I have criticized. Although it was Stendahl who advocated this division of labor between biblical scholar and theologian/pastor in his famous article on biblical theology, he did so—as Räisänen acknowledges—not in order to immunize historical-critical scholarship from critical theological reflection but in order—as Stendahl puts it—to liberate the theological enterprise from what he perceived as "the imperialism of biblical scholars" in the field of theology.[17]

Moreover, this prevalent hermeneutical division of labor between the exegete who describes what the text meant and the pastor/theologian who articulates what the text means has been seriously challenged in the past two decades and has been proven to be hermeneutically inadequate. Hence, twenty years later Stendahl poses the problem somewhat differently when he calls for scholarly attention to the "public health" aspect of biblical interpretation. Reflecting on the fact that his own exegetical-theological thinking has circled around two New Testament issues—Jews and women—he points to the clearly detrimental and dangerous effects that the bible and Christian tradition have had, as a major problem for scriptural interpretation.[18] This call for a public-ethical-political self-understanding of biblical studies has become even more pressing today after the Moral Majority in the 1970s and the Christian New Right in the 1980s and 1990s have made biblical injunctions an object of public debate.[19]

Far from seeing Stendahl as a "scientific positivist," but coming from a quite different experience and standpoint in the academy than he, I have sought as Krister Stendahl professor[20] to contribute to the articulation of such a critical ethical-political paradigm for biblical interpretation in my own work. In this regard it is not an "irony" that I occupy the Stendahl chair since my work has been consistently concerned with issues of "public health" in biblical studies.

Exploring wo/men's [21] positioning in the margins[22] of biblical scholarship and Christian theology, my work has pioneered a critical feminist biblical interpretation for liberation that is not simply accountable to the academy or to the church but to a social and religious movement for change. Such a feminist critical and evaluative interpretation for liberation seeks to recover biblical texts and biblical visions as well as the biblical past as having been shaped not just by the exclusion but also by the agency of wo/men, and it seeks to do so for the sake of wo/men in the present and the future.

Hence, a critical feminist hermeneutics cannot simply "apply" or translate the solutions of the past to the problems of the present. Rather, its historical-religious imagination seeks to reconstruct the socio-political worlds of biblical writings and contemporary biblical interpretations in order to open them up for critical inquiry and critical theological reflection. Studying the biblical past in order to name the destructive aspects of its language and symbolic universe as well as to recover its unfulfilled historical possibilities becomes a primary task for biblical scholarship today. I am sure that Krister Stendahl would not see this theoretical perspective as subverting but as extending his work although it does not subscribe to the dualistic injunction to separate "what the text meant" from "what it means" today.

To sum up my argument: I have attempted to show that Räisänen's rhetoric of marginalization seeks so to say to prove that "there is nothing new under the sun." No paradigm shift is necessary because hegemonic scholarship has already practiced for a long time what the so-called liberationists are demanding now. Hence he cites an array of established scholars in order to show that there has been no paradigm shift. Yet, if established scholars incorporate the ethics of interpretation, then what liberation scholars are saying and doing must have some legitimacy. Is Räisänen against their claim to produce new and different scholarship or is he against what they are saying or is he against both? Might it not have been better to reflect on the possibility that hegemonic scholarship could have already learned something from the "liberationists" without always giving them credit?

Since Räisänen's apologetic appeal bespeaks a refusal to engage the main challenge of my presidential address, I need to restate this challenge: I called for the decentering of hegemonic biblical scholarship not simply in terms of method but also in terms of the socializing practices of professionalization and in terms of those marginalized subjects of biblical studies who speak from different socio-cultural-religious locations. In order to clarify my proposal, I will conclude my response by sketching out major elements of the ethics of interpretation as a theoretical and institutional practice of biblical studies. Since it would require a book-length manuscript to spell out the arguments and implications of the contours of the ethics of interpretation as an intellectual discipline of biblical studies, I again refer readers to my new book *Rhetoric and Ethic: The Politics of Biblical Studies*. Here, I can only outline the ethics of interpretation in a very condensed form.

The Ethics of Interpretation

As an intellectual discipline the ethics of interpretation must be distinguished from the ethics of a text, e.g. the ethics of Paul or of the Christian (New) Testament. In my view a Christian Testament (CT) ethics investigates and systematizes the ethical or moral contents of its writings. The ethics of interpretation in turn is a second order methodological reflection on the ethos and morals of biblical studies. "Ethics" is understood here in the general sense as "morality rendered self-conscious" whereby morality names a "pervasive and often only partly conscious set of value-laden dispositions, inclinations, attitudes and habits."[23]

Thus "ethics" is best understood as a meta-theory which is critical scientific rather than positivistic scientist. As a new interdisciplinary area of critical reflexivity and research the ethics of interpretation studies the "pervasive and often only partly conscious set of value-laden dispositions, inclinations, attitudes and habits" of biblical studies as an academic discipline. Such a critical exploration of the ethos and morality of biblical scholarship, or of what it means to work scientifically and ethically, has as its goal scholarly responsibility and accountability as an integral part of the research process. In other words the ethics of interpretation seeks to articulate a professional ethics for biblical studies.

To propose the ethics of interpretation as a new interdisciplinary area in biblical studies means to overcome the assumed dichotomy between engaged scholarship (e.g. feminist, postcolonial, African-American, queer, and other sub-disciplines) and scientific (malestream) interpretation. Whereas the former is allegedly utilizing ethical criteria the latter is said to live up to a scientific ethos which gives precedence to cognitive criteria.[24] Instead I would argue that a scientific ethos demands *both* ethical and cognitive criteria which must be reasoned out in terms of inter-subjectively understandable *and* communicable knowledge. To split off rationality from ethics opens the door for irresponsible scholarship which can nevertheless from a subjective point of view be quite ethical.

The subdiscipline ethics of interpretation, I suggest, consists of the following areas of investigation:

(1) The *ethics of reading*, or of the exegesis of texts, pertains to the text and the methods used to interpret it. It investigates not only the values, norms, principles, and visions of the text, but also the value-laden assumptions and theoretical frameworks which are introduced through the chosen methods of reading. The *ethics of reading* understands:

- *Language* not as descriptive and reflective, as window to reality but as both polysemic, constructive-performative, rhetorical communicative, and as ideological misrepresentation, as marginalizing and repressive.

- *Text* as rhetorical, as inscribed communicative practices, as product of communications as determined by rhetorical situations, arguments, persuasive goals and visions. Texts are multi-voiced and tensive-conflictive.

- *Contexts* as constructed rhetorically through selection, classification, and valuation. Social contexts are produced through selection of materials, models, images, reconstruction of the social world through analogy, contrast, and imagination.

- Both the *effective history* of a text and its *communities of reading* with their norms are determining interpretation.

(2) The *ethics of interpretive practices* or scientific production has the task to critically research the process of how interpretation is produced, authorized, communicated, and used. For instance, it investigates:

- Areas of question and problem formulation.

- "Common sense" assumptions and unarticulated presuppositions.

- The lenses of reading, patterns of interpretation, categories of analysis.

- Reconstructive models, analogies, and images.

- Theoretical frameworks, world views, and points of reference.

- How the discourse of interpretation is constructed, which authorities are appealed to or which references are missing.

- Rhetoric, i.e. logos, ethos, and pathos of scientific discourses.

- Which boundaries and limits are constructed and maintained by scholarly discourses, which questions are not admitted, which arguments are silenced.

The critical reflexivity and comprehensiveness of a discourse. For instance, emancipatory interpretations are bound to be more complex and critically reflexive because they need to take both hegemonic and marginal discourses into account.

(3) The *ethics of scholarship* investigates the ethos, social location, and positionality of biblical interpretations. Who are its subjects? How are they socially located, what is their standpoint and perspective? What are the social and political values of a certain interpretation? In order to approach this question, it is necessary to develop or articulate a social-religious systemic analysis. The investigation of the unarticulated interests and goals of an interpretation is absolutely necessary in order to adjudicate its socio-political and religious functions and effects. Rhetorics, politics, and ethics are epistemologically as well as historically intertwined.

Such a scientific ethos requires an *ethics of scientific valuation and judgment* that can investigate ethical-moral norms, values, visions and ideals as well as criteria of discernment and evaluation. It explores what kind of knowledge is produced: is it technological, hermeneutic, emancipatory? Scholarship, also scholarship of the past, is always produced by and for people today with certain experiences, values, and goals. Hence, one must examine the implicit interests and unarticulated goals of scholarship, its degree of conscious responsibility and accountability. In short, if texts are polysemous and have an oppressive history of effects their interpretation always requires judgment and evaluation. Interpretation is intrinsically interested and value-laden. Hence, the criteria for adjudicating between different readings can not be just cognitive but are always also evaluative.

(4) Finally, the *ethics of communication* assesses interpretive practices as to whether they do justice not only to the text and its interpretations but also to contemporary readers, especially

to those biblical readers who are affected by biblical texts today. It analyzes scholarly interpretations as to their interests, values and visions in order to show that not only so-called engaged but also scientific supposedly value-free or value-neutral scholarship is an ideologically/theologically or ethically motivated communication.

In sum, the ethics of communication inspects biblical scholarship as an assembly of divergent communicative scientific practices. Interpretation and communication can be distinguished but they must not be dualistically separated or split off from each other as two different procedures, as interpretation and application. One can distinguish for instance between different forms or modes of communication—between scientific-technical communication (university lecture), journalistic communication (through the diverse media) everyday communication (recipes for cooking), artistic communication (poetry) or ideologically interested communication (preaching) of an interpretation but not between communication that is "scientific" and communication that is "applied," since the rhetorical process of interpretation is always already communicative i.e. intervenes in a specific communicative situation and discourse. The institutional division between scientific exegesis and ecclesial application derives from the historical-critical positivistic discourse of biblical studies as a hard science, which understood itself as "pure" objective and antiquarian exegesis free from dogmatic-ecclesiastical controls.

To sum up my argument: the ethics of interpretation seeks to re-conceptualize both biblical studies as a discipline and biblical education as its socializing practice. Insofar as biblical education still functions as socialization into the ethos of "pure," value-detached, positivistic scientism, it prohibits the institutionalization of the new paradigm. To that end the ethics of interpretation seeks to foster an ethos of critical reflexivity, democratic debate, and intellectual, "multilingual" and multidisciplinary competence. Its goal is to engender the responsible production and communication of publicly accountable scholarship. Biblical critics in the global village should not cling to outdated scholarship and scientist paradigms but actively engage in fashioning and institutionalizing the ethics of interpretation as a key-discipline of biblical studies.

I appreciate that Professor Räisänen has again brought this issue to the attention of the biblical academy and invited biblical scholars in the global village to critically engage in the ethics of interpretation.

Chapter 3

Critics, Tools, and the Global Arena

R. S. Sugirtharajah

First, I would like to thank Heikki Räisänen for his interesting essay. I am particularly pleased to see a major representative of the academy trying to interact with the hermeneutical voices which are normally regarded for their nuisance value rather than for the issues they represent. Räisänen's essay raises a number of issues. I would like to concentrate on two. One is related to the role and function of historical critical tools, and the other to the place and representation of a Third World biblical critic in a global village.

Historical Criticism and Its Role

Interestingly, the quest for the historical Jesus, the application of historical methods, and the conquest of the lands and texts and artifacts of other people, emerged in Europe more or less at the same time. I would like to make it clear that my attitude towards historical criticism is one of an ambivalence. On the one hand, I would like to affirm the historical method, and I can see its benefits, but on the other, I can see its damaging effects when it is transferred to other parts of the world and especially when it is used as a tool to conquer and subjugate other peoples' texts and stories and cultures. I need not remind the biblical scholars assembled here of the liberative nature of historical criticism when it first emerged in Europe. The method freed and relativized the absolutist theological and ecclesiastical readings of the time and made Christianity and its origins

49

and traditions earthy, questionable and humane. Those of us who are currently engaged in postcolonial criticism find the historical method helpful in decoding texts both sacred and secular, until now seen simply as innocent and symbolic but manifestly embodying values of high imperialism.

Räisänen is right, and he would concur with the Asian American cultural critic, Amy Ling, that the tools possess neither memory nor loyalty; they are as effective as the hands wielding them. Biblical interpretation brims with such instances. To take an example from the colonial archives, look at the exegetical practices of William Robertson Smith and John William Colenso. The former, a Scotsman who never ventured out of the British isles, used the then emerging high criticism to relegate the primal religions in order to vindicate the uniqueness and divine origins of the biblical religion. Critical tools enabled him to associate indigenous religions with primitive stages which were seen as being on their way to progress and civilization. The latter, an English Anglican who worked among the Zulus in South Africa, used the same tools, and what is more, used concepts from the very primal religion which Smith saw as primitive, in order to open the texts for the Zulus. Critical methods not only informed Colenso in coming up with a name for the Zulu God, but also in seeing parallels with Jews of old. What is more, for Colenso, the same Zulus provided cultural clues for reconstructing the religious practices of Israelites. More importantly, Zulu religiosity helped him to imagine God's love as a universal one, found in the sublime passages of other textual traditions such as those of the Hindu, Sikh and so forth. Colenso's commentary on the Romans combines both Western critical methods and the Zulu cultural insights, to illuminate the Pauline text for the indigenous people. I am sure there are plenty of examples in current interpretative practices as well. The crucial point is that, as Räisänen's pointed out, it is who uses the tool that's important[1].

I also see the historical method as an ally in protecting the text. A critic's role is not only to subvert and to destabilize the text, but also to protect the text against wayward readings. The text has to be protected not because of its divine propensities but because of the danger of its being read out of its historical and cultural contexts. In this task, the use of the historical critical method may not be totally disadvantageous.

Historical critical methods are invaluable for what I call creating a hermeneutics of distance. At a time when western biblical interpretation is relentlessly seeking to bridge the so-called hermeneutical gap between the text and the reader, it may come as a surprise to some that I advocate a hermeneutical distance between the text and the reader. This original sin, as I call it, and Räisänen keeps reminding up in this essay and in his other writings, is worth committing. The reason being that there is already a hermeneutics of proximity in operation in many reading communities. In an effort to interpret their lives with the help of the Bible, the tendency is to flatten the difference between the biblical world and the current situation. The fusion already exists in the ordinary readers' mind. Whenever there is a personal tragedy, it is immediately likened to that of Job's, or when faced with life threatening situations, it is assumed that they comparable to that of Daniel's situation and God's intervention is expected as in the case of the Jewish hero. The ordinary readers easily identify with bible, biblical events and biblical characters. Though existentially we may have no difficulty in seeing the relevance of the Exodus and the Exile, we must admit that these events are not about us. There is no attempt to separate biblical times and the current situation. What the historical critical method provides is a hermeneutics of distance. Any hermeneutics based on the quest for easy biblical identity is bound to produce self-righteousness. The trouble with easy identification with the biblical event, people and the motifs, is that one tends to see oneself and one's enemy in biblical stereotype: two good examples being the Zionist movement and the Afrikaners in South Africa. Such a parallelism does not give much scope for fresh dialogue and understanding. One tends to overlook the enormous political, cultural and historical differences between the present and the biblical period.

51

Though historical criticism was liberative particularly to the Western, white and middle class, it had a shackling and enslaving impact on women, blacks and people of other cultures, as the recent exegetical works of these groups have manifestly demonstrated.

To some of us the historical critical method is colonial, because of its insistence that a right reading is mediated through the proper use of historical-critical tools alone. For example, look at the opening lines of George Strecker's *The Sermon on the Mount: An Exegetical Commentary*: "No proper exegesis of the Sermon on the Mount can ignore the results of more than two hundred years of historical research into the New Testament."[2] Such a claim rules out, at the outset, the right of a reader or an interpreter to use any other means to understand the text, and those who do not practice the methods nor engage with them are seen as outside the circle and as outcastes. Moreover, such readings are seen as emotional and sentimental. The inference is that any culturally informed reading by an Asian or an African, or any politically inspired reading of a Solentiname peasant is ruled out. The peasants in Solentiname under the oppressive rule of Somoza intuitively recognized the class identity of Nicodemus, whereas David Rensberger had to plough through lexicons and commentaries to come up with the same exegetical conclusions. People with no theological training or exegetical expertise can arrive at meaning because they connect with the experience of struggle. That is to say that untrained readers arrive by intuition at a meaning which the modern scholars only reach by hard slog. In other words, because of the totalizing tendencies of the historical critical method, culturally diversified and politically informed reading will not get a look in.

Historical tools became useful to missionary educators in their relentless aim to propagate biblical faith as historical and as opposed to Hinduism which was seen as ahistorical and mythical. For establishing such a claim, historical-critical tools were seen as an appropriate pedagogical instrument and an ally. These missionary educators were passionately evangelical in introducing the intricacies of this wonderful instrument. Stanley Thoburn, a contributor to the series Indian Christian Students' Library, hailed it as a divine boon: "The scientific method is one of the greatest gifts that God has given to man, and none can deny the marvelous achievements that have come through its use."[3] The pedagogical use of historical analysis as a method of reading the Bible was the hermeneutical strategy used by the commentators in this series, in order to expose their students to the errors of their own shastras and the defects of their own philosophical systems, while simultaneously enabling them to internalize the modernist virtues of objective certitude and determinacy. An historical consciousness was seen as a necessary virtue for sifting fact from legend and as a way of establishing the factual basis of the biblical faith. Listen to the words of Anthony Hanson, the British NT scholar who started his teaching career in India, who wrote in the same series:

> We must be willing to have our Bible examined by any reasonable standard of historical criticism, because it is then that the character of Christianity founded on real historical events will stand out clearly ... On the other hand, events related in the Hindu Scriptures are found to be for the most part legend[4]

Historical tools have been used to verify the truth or falsehood of the scriptures. Different cultures have different attitudes towards their sacred writings. In certain cultures especially in India, written texts are not accorded a high status in matters of faith, and dependence upon them is viewed dimly. It may make sense to those raised in the historical critical method to ask did God create the world in seven days, or did Jesus multiply the loaves, or did he rise on the third day. But it does not make sense to a Hindu, to subject his or her texts to such historical questions as to whether stories about Rama are true or who is the author of the *Bhagavadgita*. It may be perfectly all right for Christians whose belief is rooted in history and historical accounts, to ask whether the NT references to the historical Jesus are true or not. To ask a comparable question about, say, Rama is to exhibit ignorance of other people's stories, texts and their attitude to history.

Listen to a dialogue that went on between a German writer Bichsel and an unnamed Hindu from Bali. One day the German asked the Balinese whether he "believed that the history of Prince Rama—one of the holy books of the Hindus—is true."

Without hesitation the Balinese answered "Yes."

"So you believe that the Prince Rama lived somewhere and some when?"

"I do not know if he lived," he said.

"Then it is a story?"

"Yes, it is a story."

"Then someone wrote this story—I mean: a human being wrote it?"

"Certainly some human being wrote it," he said.

"Then some human being could have also invented it." The German felt that he had triumphed, and thought that he had convinced the Indonesian.

But the Balinese said: "It is quite possible that somebody invented this story. But true it is in any case."

"Then it is the case that Prince Rama did not live on this earth."

"What is it that you want to know?" the Balinese asked. *Do you want to know whether the story is true, or merely whether it occurred?*

"The Christians believe that their God Jesus Christ was also on earth," the German said, "in the New Testament, it has been described by human beings. But the Christians believe that this is the description of the reality. Their God was really also on Earth."

The Balinese friend thought it over and said: "I had been already so informed. I do not understand why it is important that your God was on earth, but it does strike me that the Europeans are not pious. Is that correct?"

"Yes it is," said the German.

What is clear from this conversation is that the German and

the Hindu had different conceptions of truth and of history. For the young Balinese, his holy book remains true even though the narrative contents and events could have been fabricated and scripted by a human being. He does not know, and is not even interested in knowing whether Rama really lived, for it does not really affect the truth of the *Ramayana*. The historical criticism would not dream of taking a stance that would make the existence of Jesus on earth irrelevant to the truth of the Bible. The Balinese is not only drawing a distinction between a story and history but also suggesting that the historicity of the *Ramayana* is irrelevant to the story being true. But to those who are raised in Indian thought patterns, the Indian epics are not fictions, nor are they facts. Interestingly, for the Balinese, to know that the Bible is true is what makes the European impious. "Impiety is to believe that one's religion is true." To ask, which the historical critical method tends to do, whether the stories in the Indian epics are true or false is to exhibit a profound ignorance of the culture whose stories they are. To question their truth status is to assume they are knowledge items, which they are not.[5]

Second, those who engage in historical criticism, still believe in the authority of the text. The text is paramount and it becomes an object of scrutiny and investigation. Only through texts, it appears that the Bible could provide knowledge. In the West, the knowledge is believed to reside in documents and it is principally mediated through and texts, and truth's content is textual in nature. What is vital for us is not the legitimacy of a form of Christianity embedded in the text, nor a sieved-out record of the early Christian text's relationship with the original meaning of Christianity. Instead, the text has to be judged by its ability to provide avenues of resistance, emancipation and empowerment which undermine the hegemonic discourses and establishment.

Third, historical criticism was seen as a transferable pedagogic strategy to illuminate the mental darkness of Indian minds with their superstitious ways. Professor Hollenweger tells the story of John Mbiti, the first African to get a doctorate in Germany. When he went home, a great ceremony was organized to welcome him and honor his rare achievement. During the celebration a woman got possessed by a spirit. The elder said to Mbiti, "You say that you have studied the Bible in Germany. Now cast out the evil spirit in this woman." Mbiti said: "Well, you all know that I studied with Bultmann, and according to him there are no evil spirits. He has demythologized all." When the crowd heard this, they said, "What is the use of studying in Europe? Before, you could heal. Now you can't."

Biblical criticism as it is practiced today lends support to the hypothesis that, if a reader is not conversant with the latest critical scholarship, it is his or her fault. With its exotic methods, constant shifting of scholarly opinions, and continual revision of the periodization of biblical history, the critical enterprise has become living proof of Bernard Shaw's dictum that every profession is a conspiracy against the laity. What Joseph Parker wrote in the early days, about what then was known as the higher criticism, still rings true:

> I am jealous lest the Bible should in any sense be made a priest's book. Even Baur or Colenso may contrary to his own wishes, be almost unconsciously elevated into a literary deity under whose approving nod alone we can read the Bible with edification. It is no secret that when Baur rejected the Epistle to the Philippines as un-Pauline, Christian Europe became partially paralyzed, and that when Hilgenfeld pronounced it Pauline Christian Europe resumed its prayers. Do we have to wait a communication from Tübingen, or a telegram from Oxford, before we can read the Bible?[6]

The speed with which scholarship is moving these days can make one feel miserably outdated. In a culture which instantly prostrates before the cult of the latest, biblical scholarship is responsible for those numbers swelling. Whether the latest scholarly theory has any relevance to the context is seldom addressed.

Added to this is over specialization in the field, which has resulted in, what Said, calls the "cult of professional expertise." The relentless engagement in fruitless historical pursuits, and theories has made biblical scholars marginal to what is going on in their own societies. Said's solution is fully applicable to biblical scholars as well. He calls for an amateurism of approach which does away with "priestly" and abstruse speculations, and advocates engagement in worldly causes:

> However much intellectuals pretend that their representations are of higher things or ultimate values, morality begins with their activity in this secular world of ours—where it takes place, whose interests it serves, how it jibes with a consistent and universalistic ethic, how it discriminates between power and justice, what it reveals of one's choices and priorities.[7]

What is needed is a type of critical practice that will not only go beyond the literary-historical activity, but will place scholarship well within the grasp of the reading public, and will significantly place scholarship at the service of the people and their day-to-day social and political concerns.

The Global Village and Third World Biblical Critics

The problem for us in the global village is not what we do with the historical criticism, its usefulness or its non-usefulness. There are concerns that are missing in Räisänen's essay. What concerns Third World hermeneuts is the systematic editing out of their work. Mainstream scholarship often acted repressively and prohibitively towards Third World biblical discourse. What I see here is the hermeneutical strategy of negation at work here. David Spurr, who has mapped out the different rhetorical strategies of Western thinking to deal with other cultures, defines negation as a strategy

> by which Western writing conceives of the Other as absence, emptiness, nothingness, or death. This exploration leads to the formulation of two principles; first, negation serves to reject the ambiguous object for which language and experience provide no adequate framework of interpretation; second, . . . negation acts as a kind of provincial erasure, clearing a space for the expansion of the colonial imagination and the pursuit of desire.[8]

The efforts of Asian and African and Latin American thinkers during the colonial period and later are either ignored or seen as not worthy of any serious attention by western biblical scholars. There is a tendency to overlook the long tradition of biblical interpretation. I have in mind some of the efforts of the Indians during the Empire days. There are comparable examples in other countries as well. For instance, even long before Albert Schweitzer embarked on the modern search for the historical Jesus, Raja Rammohun Roy was engaged in such a task, although he did not identify his investigation in those terms. In his *Precepts of Jesus: The Guide to Peace and Happiness* (1820), employing his own version of the reader response criticism which is currently in vogue in biblical scholarship, he was indeed searching for a historical Jesus who was a moral guide. Hong Xiuquan's rework of Mark's gospel during the Taiping revolution; Matsumura Kaiseki's editing out of canonical material and the production of his own version known as the Dokkai Bible; the appropriation of the Bible by the Harrist and Aladura movements, and the hermeneutical presuppositions of such attempts, were overlooked or side-lined. Unfortunately, the efforts of these people were not seen as sophisticated enough to be studied within biblical disciplines, but were relegated to church history, mission studies or practical theology and not offered their proper place in biblical studies. My intention is not to be triumphalistic and say that we in the Third World attempted all these hermeneutical pursuits, but to serve as a reminder that there is a long tradition of biblical discourse which has been eclipsed not only by the dominant biblical scholarship in the West but sadly also by our Third World theological institutions.

The current changing scenario at the global level has serious implications for Third World hermeneutics. First, there is a slow but perceptible fragmentation of Western theologies. The Western theologies which invaded our space, and took upon themselves the mantle to speak for all, and have lost their nerve. This has occurred either through postmodern fragmentation or through vigorous internal critiquing. Western theologies have become more regional, autobiographical and confessional. A typical example is the recent issue of *Semeia* on autobiographical criticism, wherein every contributor started by stating his or her social location, sexuality, and the constituency which she or he was aiming at or addressing. If hermeneutics is seen as something personal and an isolated enterprise, where then is the room for dialogue and mutual critiquing. Third world hermeneutics, especially the liberation variety, arose as a way of critiquing the universalistic and eurocentric, individualistic, patriarchal, and anti-environmental tendencies of these western theologies. Now we have been pushed further to the periphery in the name of postmodern celebration of the local and the different.

The second implication for Third World hermeneutics is the postmodern prohibition against subject-centered inquiry. Postmodernism, among other things is suspicious of representation, agency and self identity. Why is it that, at a time when previously silenced people have began to script their own stories and speak for themselves, the West celebrates the death of the author and proclaims that the mega-stories are over. The West is currently experiencing the loss of grand discourse and is frowning at the idea of the power of agency, at a time when the subalterns are trying to make their stories heard. The *Postmodern Bible* produced by the cultural collective, with its under-estimation of grand stories and unsigned articles, is an example of the current trend in the West. At a time when postcolonial theorists are trying to recover subaltern histories and stories, we are informed that there is no history to be narrated or stories to be told.

Finally, Räisänen's essay passionately calls for ethical interpretation and the involvement of the biblical critic in the ongoingness of life. I have no problem with that and I warmly support it, but at the same time, I would like to acknowledge that we as biblical critics have only a limited role. Sometimes we become grandiose about our function and aims. Theologians often assume the role of legislators, and expect that their hermeneutical treaties will change the world. The task of the hermeneut is not to change the world but to understand it. Hermeneutics does not create revolution; it changes people's perceptions and makes them aware of the need for revolution. Its function is to make people see more, feel more, rekindle the fire of resistance.

Chapter 4

Dethroning Biblical Imperialism in Theology

Krister Stendahl

What can I say here? Having first been identified as the chief sinner and then so graciously redeemed, what can I add? Heikki Räisänen and I are in strong agreement about how indispensable our type of critical historical scholarship is for both academy, church, and society at large[1]—not only in the West.[2] Independently of each other we have also gravitated to what I think is *the* most crucial challenge to the Christian theology in the years ahead: How to shape a Christian theology of religions, and how to find the proper role of biblical studies in that creative task. With the publication of his Cadbury Lectures at the University of Birmingham, *Marcion, Muhammad and the Mahatma: Exegetical Perspectives on the Encounter of Cultures and Faiths,*[3] Räisänen is a pioneer in that quest. I rejoice that he now has chosen to place that quest at the top of our agenda.

Since I agree so firmly with his basic claims, it would be artificial for me to frame my response as a critique. Rather allow me some comments and observations about, around, and possibly beyond his presentation.

My first observation is that Räisänen calls a spade a spade. There is no defensiveness on behalf of the Bible. I like that. I have long felt that apologetics often is the lowest form of theology. To defend God strikes me as quite arrogant. Look who is defending whom. As the Swedes say, "It is pathetic to hear mosquitoes cough," and apologetics activates the least creative drive in our souls.

Two quotes from his *Marcion, Muhammad and the Mahatma* demonstrate well his non-apologetic stance: "One should face the possibility that curious (and problematic) ideas may also be found even in central places in the Bible" (6). "One should in fact be free to decide against all biblical options if need be" (202). The "troubling texts" must be allowed to challenge us in their fullest form. Like Räisänen, I am fond of referring to Jon Levenson's article "Is There a Counterpart in the Hebrew Bible to New Testament Antisemitism?"[3] There the Amalek texts and motif are faced in all their gory problematic. This is not even a hermeneutics of suspicion. The troubling texts are not "suspect." They are clearly offensive and call for unapologetic hermeneutical response.

Since Räisänen has lifted up my distinction between "what it meant" and "what it means," it is tempting for me to turn autobiographical, and perhaps that may be allowed to an old man. Räisänen is right in seeing that my hermeneutical move was aimed at dethroning the theological imperialism that biblical scholars often enjoyed, or presumed, in the heyday of Biblical Theology.[6] In my case that aim was quite specific. As has often been noticed, the basic hermeneutical stance of bible scholars can be best understood as a response to the one issue that first forced them to take a stand. That is certainly true for me. Let me be quite up front about it even if, to some, this might limit the validity of the method.

The issue was the ordination of women in the Church of Sweden. And the triggering factor was the signing of a public statement to be signed by the New Testament teachers in Uppsala and Lund Universities. They declared ordination of women to the priesthood to be contrary to the Bible—with no if, and, or but! It was the early 1950s. I was a doctoral student at the time, also part of the teaching staff. When asked to sign, I found myself in a strange position. I was quite convinced that the ordination of women was the right thing, and that for many reasons. At the same time I found the arguments of my teachers and colleagues exegetically sound. I did not want to make Paul and/or Jesus into proto-feminists. Certainly the overwhelming biblical perception of the role of women could not easily be brushed aside, for example by reference to those docile women in Luke's gospel. I had to give reasons for not signing on, and when you are in a minority of one, you have to think harder. Hence the urgent need to take the hermeneutical gap more seriously.

To counteract the imperialism of biblical scholars I assigned to them/us the limited role of what I called the descriptive task. I am now more aware that also description is an imaginative and creative task.[5] But I remain critical of those who use the impossibility of objectivity as a license for not trying, and for not raising questions, like: What did Paul mean, or think, or intend—or think that he thought? And what did the recipients of his epistles hear him say? Nor does the stating of one's presuppositions, what now is called "where I come from," dispense the scholar from that descriptive task, however imaginative the descriptive process might be.

The more clearly the primary role of biblical scholars were limited to their giving access to "original" meanings, the greater the need for the other members of the theological team, not least creative systematic theologians.

A ruthless pursuit of the descriptive task does not preclude an awareness of the world as we experience it. To the contrary, it unmasks those elements in the Scriptures that have caused and do cause harm, what I like to call the undesirable side effects of our holy medicine. That metaphor makes me a member of the "department of public health" within the theological enterprise, perhaps too much leaving the role of surgeons—the evangelicals—and internists—the main line denominations—to others.

In his writings Räisänen uses the expression "reading against the grain."[7] Also in that respect we have come to make similar moves. To me it became important to question all homogenizing readings and develop a keen eye for the moves or asides or afterthoughts that went against the often overwhelmingly consistent views that dominate the Scriptures, be the questions christological or anthropological. And Gal 3:28 became a case in point: "There is neither Jew nor Greek, there is neither slave nor free, *there is not 'male and female'*." To begin with, most translators seem to ignore the change of syntax in the third link of this famous tripartite statement of the radical implications of baptism. By making a straight quotation of Gen 1:27, the point of transcending the gender dichotomy is made the more powerful.

It is also worth noting that the issue that dominates the letter to the Galatians—and especially its third chapter—is the Judaizing among the Gentiles—and the slave/free and male/female examples are corroborating analogies, just as Jews/Gentiles and slave/free have that function in Paul's answer to the Corinthian inquiry about sexual relations, about marriage and celibacy, divorce and breaking engagements (1 Cor 7). Thus my assessment was and is that Paul speaks *malgré lui*, almost in spite of himself in Gal 3:28. He is carried away theologically beyond his own perception and his own patterns of society. In short, he is a better theologian than a social ethicist. When contemplating how in baptism all dichotomies are transcended, Paul reaches all the way back to the primordial divide of male and female. It surely goes "against the grain" of even his own thinking. The hermeneutical point is this: Let not such elements be smothered or neutralized. Exactly since they do not fit, they indicate sensitivities, caveats, second thoughts, and hence so far unexploited resources for the tasks of theology.

The Galatian example may be considered a covert, perhaps unconscious case of "against the grain," as I like to use that term. One of the most overt and clear such cases is Paul's letter to the Romans 11:11–36. I refer to the way in which Paul warns his Gentile protégées against superiority feelings toward Israel. As I read the text he finds their sense of superiority to be not only unwarranted but a troubling sign of a "secular" missiology. They are insensitive to the mysterious ways of God. And it is striking that this section (ch. 9–11) of Romans— which

I consider the nucleus of the epistle—ends in a doxology without any reference to Jesus Christ. It is the only Pauline doxology where that is the case. I think it is important to note that.

Thus Paul is the first Christian[9] theologian who discerned the potentiality of Christian antisemitism in particular and missionary arrogance in general.[8] It is tempting to ask How come? It goes certainly "against the grain" of much of his writing. In his zealous defense for the place and rights of his converts he was capable of invectives like "dogs" and his tasteless calumny exploiting the image of circumcision is well known (Gal 3:2). He certainly was not bashful about the name of Christ. So, how come? Could it be that he had been burned once? It was out of missionary zeal that he had committed the only sin he ever confesses: he had persecuted the Church of God (1 Cor 15:9, Gal 1:13, Phil 3:6). His *déjà vu* made him sensitive to the potentially "undesirable side effects" of his own gospel. He perceived the possibility that it would happen again— as it did. Oh that we had heard and heeded his warnings.

To me it became increasingly important to widen the gap between original meanings and what came to be or what may now be the meanings, often driven by moral sensitivities and insights not found in the text. And it became equally urgent to discern the tensions within the Scriptures, not least when an author seemed to have second thoughts. In those tensions and second thoughts I found pointers toward alternatives. Awareness of "the road not taken"[10] reopened many a case in the history of church and society. Perhaps I became too preoccupied with what had gone wrong with those undesirable side affects, and with those "troubling texts." While feeling that I was helping in the task of unmasking all kinds of Western male and racial imperialisms I now must ask to what extent the very method I championed was in itself so wedded to Western culture that it was actually part of the post-colonial problematic. Perhaps something happened to me similar to what is said to happen in the education of lawyers: By constantly concentrating on the "hard cases" their moral sense is weakened or skewed. And yet, it is hard for me to think of a time and place in which curiosity and honesty would not force a twenty-first century reader of the Bible to ask questions like: What did Paul have in mind when he wrote, "For salvation is closer to us now than when we first believed" (Rom 13:11)?

Appendix 1

Biblical Theology, Contemporary

Krister Stendahl

[Note: This text is reproduced from *The Interpreter's Dictionary of the Bible*, 4 vols. (Nashville: Abingdon Press, 1962), 1:418–32, with the permission of Abingdon Press. It has been edited slightly for inclusion in the present volume, and the original bibliography has been omitted.]

A historical survey of major contributions to the field of biblical theology, such as in "Biblical Theology, History of" [in the *IDB*] makes it more than obvious that there is no one definition of this field on which biblical scholars can unanimously agree. It is true that a closer analysis of contemporary contributions to the field may well show that some of the older definitions are obsolete, as well as bring to light certain common tendencies in aim and method; but it will not eliminate the tensions between different conceptions of what a biblical theology is or should be. Such diversity was to be expected, since very different theological and philosophical presuppositions are necessarily involved.

And yet, in spite of these differences, recent biblical studies have gravitated with an unprecedented enthusiasm toward topics and problems which undoubtedly fall within the biblical theological field. This seems to be due to the fact that a new stage has been set for biblical theology, as a result of a new emphasis upon its descriptive task. Since consideration of this task has proved far more suggestive and creative than is often recognized, there is good reason to consider the nature of the new descriptive biblical theology and then to move toward its implications for other aspects of theology. This can be done only by way of hermeneutics. Thus we arrive at the following outline:

A. The descriptive task
    1. A new stage set for biblical theology
    2. What it meant and what it means
    3. Three approaches to NT theology
        a. Barth
        b. Bultmann
        c. Cullmann
        d. Conclusions
    4. Is a descriptive NT theology possible?
    5. The descriptive approach and the OT
    6. "Sacred history" and the unity of the Bible
B. The hermeneutic question
    1. As raised by a descriptive biblical theology
    2. Alternative answers to the hermeneutic question
    3. The significance of "canon" for biblical theology
    4. The preacher and biblical theology

A. The Descriptive Task

1. A new stage set for biblical theology. The alleged biblical basis for what has been called "liberal theology" in its classical form (the use of the term "liberal" in this sense, referring to the dominant theology ca. 1900, does not imply that many more recent types of theology are not just as "liberal" in their method and presuppositions) —i.e., the view that the OT is a witness to the evolution of a more and more ethical monotheism and that the gospels are biographies of Jesus as the even more refined teacher of the Golden Rule, the fatherhood of God, and the eternal value of the individual—the alleged biblical basis of this view was not shattered by the conservatives, but by the extreme radicals of the *religionsgeschichtliche Schule* ("history-of-religions school"; *see* "Biblical Criticism" [in the *IDB*]). They could show, on the basis of the comparative material, that such a picture of Jesus or of the OT prophets was totally impossible from a historical point of view and that it told more about the ideals of bourgeois Christianity in the late nineteenth century than about the carpenter from Nazareth or the little man from Tekoa. What emerged out of the studies of the *religions-geschichtliche Schule* was a new picture of the men, the ideas, and the institutions of biblical history. Those elements and traits, which did strike modern man as crude, primitive, cultic, and even magical, were now given equal and often greater emphasis than those which happened to appeal to enlightened Western taste. The "peril of modernizing Jesus"—to use Henry J. Cadbury's phrase—was fully recognized. Johannes Weiss and Albert Schweitzer made a forceful plea for a most abstruse and appalling eschatology as the actual setting for Jesus and his followers; H. Gunkel, H. Gressmann, and S. Mowinckel placed the OT back in the matrix of Near Eastern myth and cult. Johannes Pedersen applied V. Groenbech's studies of human self-understanding in old Nordic religion to an extensive study of OT anthropology, where cherished distinctions between soul and body, magic and religion, cult and ethics, individual and collective, were thoroughly intermingled and lost much of their meaning. It became a scholarly ideal to creep out of one's Western and twentieth-century skin and identify oneself with the feelings and thought-patterns of the past. The distance between biblical times and modern times was stressed, and the difference between biblical thought and systematic theology became much more than that of diversification over against systematization or of concrete exemplification over against abstract propositions.

What emerged was a descriptive study of biblical thought—empathetic in the sense that it was beyond sympathy or antipathy. This was actually a new phenomenon in biblical studies, and yet it came as a mature outgrowth of the historical and critical study of the Scriptures. It differed in three ways from earlier contributions of historical criticism:

(a) The strait jacket of doctrinaire evolutionism—in Darwinistic as well as in Hegelian terms—was considerably loosened. While development and stages were recognized and noticed, the later stages were not preconceived as progression (e.g., from priests to prophets) or regression (e.g., from Jesus to Paul). Each period and each ideology was given enough attention to be granted a careful description on its own terms.

(b) The question of fact—i.e., whether, e.g., the march through the Red Sea or the resurrection of Jesus had actually taken place as described—was not any more the only one which absorbed the historian. Now there was more concern about what the function and the significance of such an item or of such a message as "He is risen" might have been to the writers and readers (or hearers) of the biblical records. Form criticism and *Sitz im Leben* became the catchwords for students of the documents of temple, synagogue, and church.

(c) The question about relevance for present-day religion and faith was waived, or consciously kept out of sight. This statement will be, perhaps, the strongest reminder of how biblical theology was swallowed up or threatened by a history of biblical thought or a history of biblical religion. This historicism or antiquarianism, with its lack of interest in relevance, has been challenged on many scores by modern writers. And yet it remains a fact that modern biblical theology would be quite inexplicable were it not for the fact that the *religionsgeschichtliche Schule* had drastically widened the hiatus between our time and that of the Bible, between West and East, between the questions self-evidently raised in modern minds and those presupposed, raised and answered in the Scriptures. Thereby a radically new stage was set for biblical interpretation. The question of meaning was split up in two tenses: "What *did* it mean?" and "What *does* it mean?" These questions were now kept apart long enough for the descriptive task to be considered in its own right.

2. What it meant and what it means. To liberals and conservatives alike, this distinction was not sharply in focus prior to the *religionsgeschichtliche Schule*. We may be justified in taking Harnack's *What Is Christianity?* as the most influential popular summary of liberal interpretation of the NT. It is not accidental that Harnack, as Bultmann points out in his Introduction to a reprint of the work (1950), "failed to realize the importance of the so-called *religionsgeschichtliche Schule* and never truly became sympathetic with it." Albert Schweitzer had brought this aspect of Harnack's interpretation to bear upon the problem now under consideration when he said in *The Quest of the Historical Jesus:* "Harnack in his 'What Is Christianity?' almost entirely ignores the contemporary limitations of Jesus' teaching, and starts out with a Gospel which carries him down without difficulty to the year 1899."

The apologetic intentions of the "liberals" should not be forgotten. In the light of later development, "liberal" came to stand for the "leftists" in the theological assembly. By the turn of the century this was not so. The liberals understood themselves as the mediating party who, often with a deep concern for Christianity and its future role in our culture and with a genuine piety, refuted the radical assaults of D. F. Strauss and others. But the way in which they carried on their apologetic task make them poor historians of religion. Their methods were basically the same as those used by the conservatives. Both were convinced that the Bible contained revelation which could be grasped in the clean form of eternal truth unconditioned and uncontaminated by historical limitations. The difference was only one of degree. While the orthodox interpreters found this revelation in the whole of scripture and systematized it by harmonization and by interpreting the less easily fitting by those passages which were hand in glove with their own systems, the liberals arrived at the pure revelation by way of more or less drastic reductions. This reductionist approach was often carried out by literary criticism, but once the *ipsissima verba* ("very words") of the prophets or of Jesus were established, these words happened to square well with the ideals of the modern age. Thus the tension between the past and the present meaning had been overcome before it could create any problems for interpretation. And this happened because the liberals were convinced that the teachings of the Bible were meaningful for modern man—just as the orthodox claimed the same for a vastly more challenging amount of biblical teaching.

71

For the liberals the nucleus of revelation had to be that which could be hailed as relevant and acceptable to modern man.

The resistance to the *religionsgeschichtliche Schule* was openly or unconsciously aimed against its disregard for theological meaning and relevance. By and large, Gunkel's *Schöpfung und Chaos in Urzeit und Endzeit,* Mowinckel's *Psalmenstudien,* and Schweitzer's *Quest* appeared on the scene with no immediate relation to the ongoing theological discussion. Schweitzer's work did actually contain an Epilogue in which the author made a cautious attempt to draw out the ramifications of the thoroughgoing eschatology of Jesus for theology as well as for the life of the believer, but the return is rather small. When facing the shocking distance back to the Jesus of the gospels, Schweitzer finally takes refuge in an expectant mysticism where the Christ of faith comes to us as "One unknown," yet One who in an ineffable mystery lets man experience who He is. In the German edition this final sentence of the whole volume symbolically ends with ellipsis dots.

This ellipsis formed, however, a challenge, the response to which is the vigorous interest in biblical theology starting in the 1920s and showing no slackening tendencies toward the end of the 1950s. Once freed from the anachronistic interpretations of their predecessors, and forced to accept the hiatus between the ideas and ideals in the biblical material, the theologically minded student of the Scriptures slowly found a new and deeper relevance in what the *religionsgeschichtliche Schule* described for him as the pre-Westernized meaning of sayings and events. In the broader context of cultural climate this tendency had its obvious similarities in the taste for the primitive, with its crude vigor in art, music, and literature. It was akin to Rudolf Otto's reevaluation of religious phenomena in his study of holiness. It had striking parallels in the field of historical theology, where, e.g., Luther's own words and intentions were sharply contrasted with the teaching of seventeenth-century Lutheranism, the sympathies of the scholars always siding with the former. But it was primarily the experience of the distance and the strangeness of biblical thought as a creative asset, rather than as a destructive and burdensome liability.

Without this new nonmodernizing look at the Bible, Karl Barth's programmatic commentary on Romans or Rudolph Bultmann's *Theology of the NT*—or his book written in 1926 on Jesus—would be inexplicable. O. Cullmann's *Christ and Time*, as well as his more recent *NT Christology*, are the typical examples of a somewhat different result of the same ideal of historical distance. In OT studies, W. F. Albright's *From the Stone Age to Christianity* and G. E. Wright's *God Who Acts*, as well as W. Eichrodt's and G. von Rad's OT theologies, are all inspired by the same tension between the mind of a Semitic past and the thought of modern man. Yet most of these writers launch strong attacks on the "historicism" of the "historian of religion." By these terms they do, however, usually refer to other elements in the *religionsgeschichtliche Schule* than the one to which attention has been drawn here—viz., the descriptive element, and its awareness of the distinction between what it meant and what it means.

3. Three approaches to NT theology. This distinction between past and present meaning has its specific problems for OT theology, and we may consequently be wise in first trying to clarify the issue in relation to NT theology: Karl Barth, Rudolf Bultmann, and Oscar Cullmann. They are all aware of what we have called the distance between the centuries. Especially Bultmann's relation to the radical tradition—over against the liberal—in biblical studies is obvious—e.g., in his references to D. F. Strauss. The question raised by the distance should thus be faced in its most radical form: Do these old documents have any meaning for us—except as sources for our knowledge of a small segment of first-century life and thought, or as means for a nostalgic visit to the first era of Christian history? If they have a meaning in the present tense and sense, on what ground do they have this meaning?

a. Barth. In the preface to the second edition of his commentary on Romans, Barth argues for the exegesis of Luther and Calvin over against that of men like Jülicher and

Lietzmann. The former are the only ones who really have tried to "understand" Paul, since, e.g., Calvin, "having first established what stands in the text, sets himself to re-think the whole material and to wrestle with it, till the walls which separate the sixteenth century from the first become transparent, i.e., till Paul *speaks* there and the man of the sixteenth century *hears* here, till the conversation between the document and the reader is totally concentrated on the subject-matter, which *cannot* be a different one in the first and sixteenth century." The concentration on the subject matter (God, Jesus, grace, etc.) bridges the gap between the centuries, and does so since they cannot but be the same. This identity in the subject matter guarantees the meaningfulness of the Pauline writings. They must speak about what Calvin (or the modern interpreter) knows as the subject matter. This is apparently so since God, Christ, and all of revelation stand above history. Thereby the tension between the first century and ours is resolved, or rather transformed, into a theological category of "otherness."

It is also significant to note that Barth speaks as if it were a very simple thing to establish what Paul actually meant in his own terms. To say that the Reformers interpreted Paul by equating the problem of the Judaizers and the Torah in Paul with the problem of work-righteousness in late medieval piety and that this ingenious translation or application of Pauline theology may be 80 percent correct but left 20 percent of Paul inexplicable—and consequently distorted in a certain sense the true picture of Pauline thought—to say this is to call attention to a problem which could not be detected, let alone criticized, by Barth or any truly Barthian exegete. Thus biblical theology along this line is admittedly incapable of enough patience and enthusiasm for keeping alive the tension between what the text meant and what it means. There are no criteria by which they can be kept apart; what is intended as a commentary turns out to be a theological tractate, expanding in contemporary terms what Paul should have said about the subject matter as understood by the commentator.

When the term "biblical theology" is used of works where

this method is applied, it does not designate anything basically different from systematic theology, except that its systematic task is so defined as to make the Bible central in its work. Thus it may be convenient for classification within the realm of systematic theology to speak of this theology as "biblical" rather than philosophical. But from the point of view of biblical studies such a theology is not automatically "more biblical" than other types of systematic theology.

b. Bultmann. On the last page of Bultmann's *Theology of the NT* we find a statement (in italics below), apparently made in passing, which is worth noting in relation to the question if or why the biblical documents have any meaning for the present. He places the reader before an alternative: "Either the writings of the NT can be interrogated as the 'sources' to reconstruct a picture of primitive Christianity as a phenomenon of the historical past, or the reconstruction stands in the service of the interpretation of the NT writings *under the presupposition that they have something to say for the present."* Bultmann sides with the second alternative, and in so doing he takes for granted that the NT has such meaning. For Bultmann, as for Barth, the common denominator of meaning is the subject matter; but for Bultmann there is only one subject matter which is valid: human self-understanding as it expresses itself in the NT and as it is experienced through human history until the present time. This gives to his NT theology a strikingly uneven character. In dealing with the message of Jesus, the kerygma of the early church and its development into the second century, his method is by and large descriptive; but in the exposition of Pauline and Johannine material—and this is almost half the whole work—the tone and even the method are different, since these writings lend themselves so much more easily to anthropological interpretation.

Yet nobody could blame Bultmann for not having given reasons for what he is doing. Most of his later writings have centered around his plea for demythologizing, and it has become more and more obvious that this to Bultmann also implies a dehistoricizing of the NT. His attack on the historicism of

NT interpretation (i.e., the use of the NT as a 'source' for our knowledge of a historical past, be it the historical Jesus or the life and teaching of early Christianity) is centered in his emphasis on the NT as a message, a kerygma. The intent of NT theological utterances is not to state a doctrine (as for orthodoxy) and not to give the material for a concept (as treated by the historians). It is to challenge man in his own self-understanding, and consequently "the act of thinking must not be divorced from the act of living." When the NT kerygma witnesses to historical events (as in 1 Cor 15:3–8), these "events" are of little significance as events: what counts is to recreate their effect on man's self-understanding. Thus—in Bultmann's own view—his NT theology becomes "theology" explicitly only where it clarifies the "believing self-understanding in its reference to the kerygma." As such—and only as such—has the NT "something to say to the present." Only on such terms does Bultmann find it possible to do justice to the intent of the NT.

c. Cullmann. In Cullmann, perhaps the most productive contemporary writer in the field of NT theology, we find a very different approach to biblical theology. If history is mute to Bultmann for reasons of hermeneutics and philosophy—a view which colors Bultmann's exegesis to the extent that he interprets NT eschatology as implying the end of history in Christ—Cullmann finds the key to NT theology in its understanding of time. Most discussions of Cullmann's *Christ and Time* have centered around a criticism of his distinction of linear time (biblical) versus circular time (Greek) and his idea of Christ as the center of time, but if these interpretations were refuted, the thrust of Cullmann's argument is still unchallenged when it urges us to recognize how the categories of time and history, rather than essence, nature, and eternal or existential truth, are the ones within which the NT moves (cf. Cullmann's "Le mythe dans les écrits du NT," *Numen* 1 [1954]: 120–35). Cullmann has thereby recaptured the mood of thought of the NT writers and stays within it long enough to work out its implication for different aspects of NT thought. On the other hand, it is not quite clear how Cullmann understands the relation between such a descriptive biblical theology in its first and second-century terms and its translation into our present age; his hermeneutic discussions have nothing of the radical penetration of Bultmann's. His work is basically confined to the descriptive task, and when Bultmann could say about Cullmann—as he does about E. Stauffer's NT theology—that he "transforms theology into a religious philosophy of history," Cullmann's answer would be that NT theology *is*, whether we like it or not, a religious philosophy of history, and that he finds it difficult to see how this historical dimension can be translated away in any presentation of the gospel to the present age.

Such a discussion between Cullmann, Stauffer, and Bultmann would, however, be totally fruitless, for the following reasons: (a) All three take for granted that the NT has "meaning," but while Bultmann discusses from a vantage point of his own motivation for such a meaning, Cullmann (and Stauffer) have not clarified their answer to why or how they consider the NT as meaningful for the present age. Because of this lack of clarification, their works are read by many—perhaps most—readers as being on the same level of present meaning as Bultmann's or Barth's highly "translated" interpretations: and there are indications that they do not mind such a use of their works. A close study of Stauffer's NT theology makes it quite clear, however, that its method remains strictly descriptive; this is the more obvious in his extensive and impressive use of non-canonical intertestamental material as equally significant to picture the mood of NT thought. Cullmann's Christology follows suit in this respect. (b) Consequently, Bultmann's critique of such an approach should be the opposite to what it actually is. He could charge his opponents with not having seen the need which he himself has epitomized in his quest for demythologizing. This would force his opponents to clarify why they consider such a dehistoricizing translation unnecessary or arbitrary. (c) Bultmann's case for the end of history in Christ and Cullmann's for ongoing history as the essence of NT eschatology have to be tested on the descriptive level. On this level a meaningful discussion can be carried on. If Cullmann seems to be much closer to the truth, Bultmann's interpretations may remain valid as a demythologized translation. But the "validity" of such an interpretation hinges then on the validity of the hermeneutic principles of the interpreter, and is of no direct consequence to the descriptive task of biblical theology.

In the present state of biblical studies, Cullmann's (and Stauffer's) contribution reminds us of Schweitzer, who felt himself compelled to present as forceful an eschatological picture of Jesus as he found in the sources, in spite of the fact he did not see too clearly what its theological ramifications might be. This is the same as saying that these works carry the signs of hope which belong to every vigorous contribution to descriptive biblical theology, in spite of hermeneutic unclarity. The pitfall for both the scholars and the common reader is the ambiguity by which the descriptive method is allowed to transcend its own limitations. (Stauffer later moved on to a quite different methodology, by which he claims to have established a new basis for the "historical Jesus.")

d. Conclusions. It thus appears that the tension between "what it meant" and "what it means" is of a competitive nature, and that when the biblical theologian becomes primarily concerned with the present meaning, he implicitly (Barth) or explicitly (Bultmann) loses his enthusiasm or his ultimate respect for the descriptive task. And yet the history of the discipline indicates that all types of biblical theology depend on the progress of this descriptive biblical theology, to which the contribution of the theologically irrelevant representatives of the *religionsgeschichtliche Schule* is strikingly great.

From the very beginning of the use of the term "biblical theology" in the seventeenth century, there has been the tension between the contemporary (be it scholasticism, conservatism, liberalism, or existentialism) and the biblical, but it is in the light of historical criticism that this tension has become clarified as one between two centuries with drastically different modes of thought. Once this difference became great enough to place the Bible further away from us—to the liberal theology the historical Jesus was closer to modern man than was the Christ confessed in the dogma of the church—the need for "translation" became a real one. Bultmann's plea for demythologizing—regardless of the way in which he carries it out—is certainly here to stay. But this makes it the more imperative to have the "original" spelled out with the highest degree of perception in its own terms. This is the nucleus of all biblical theology, and the way from this descriptive task to an answer about the meaning in the present cannot be given in the same breath on an *ad hoc* basis. It presupposes an extensive and intensive competence in the field of hermeneutics. With the original in hand, and after due clarification of the hermeneutic principles involved, we may proceed toward tentative answers to the question of the meaning here and now. But where these three stages become intermingled, there is little hope for the Bible to exert the maximum of influence on theology, church life, and culture. How much of the two last stages should belong to the discipline of biblical studies or to what extent they call for teamwork with the disciplines of theology and philosophy is a practical question, a question which in itself indicates the nature of the problem. If the three stages are carelessly intermingled, the theology as well as the preaching in our churches becomes a mixed or even an inarticulate language.

4. Is a descriptive NT theology possible? Many are those who express serious doubts about the possibility of the descriptive task as pictured above. Every historian is subjective in the selection of his material, and it is often said that he does more harm when he thinks himself to be objective—i.e., when he does not recognize, not to say openly state, what his presuppositions and preconceived ideas are. We can smile when we see how an earlier generation of biblical scholars peddled Kantian, Hegelian, or Ritschlian ideas, all the time subjectively convinced that they were objective scholars who only stated "facts." All this naturally calls for caution; but the relativity of human objectivity does not give us an excuse to excel in bias, not even when we state our bias in an introductory chapter.

What is more important, however, is that once we confine ourselves to the task of descriptive biblical theology as a field in its own right, the material itself gives us means to check weather our interpretation is correct or not. To be sure, the sources are not extensive enough to allow us certainty in all areas; and the right to use some comparative material, while disregarding other such material as irrelevant for our texts, gives further reason for uncertainty; but from the point of view of method it is clear that our only concern is to find out what these words meant when uttered or written by the prophet, the priest, the evangelist, or the apostle and regardless of their meaning in later stages of religious history, our own included. Such a progress is by and large a new feature in biblical studies, a mature fruit of the historical method. It does not necessarily disregard the intent of the biblical texts, but captures the implication of their kerygmatic nature when it lifts them out of the framework of "theological concepts" and places them back into their *Sitz im Leben* (the "life situation") of Israel or the church.

This descriptive task can be carried out by believer and agnostic alike. The believer has the advantage of automatic empathy with the believers in the text—but his faith constantly threatens to have him modernize the material, if he does not exercise the canons of descriptive scholarship rigorously. The agnostic has the advantage of feeling no such temptations, but his power of empathy must be considerable if he is to identify himself sufficiently with the believer of the first century. Yet both can work side by side, since no other tools are called for than those of description in the terms indicated by the texts themselves. The meaning for the present—in which the two interpreters are different—is not involved, and thus total cooperation is possible, and part of their mutual criticism is to watch whether concerns for meaning or distaste for meaning colors the descriptions where it should not.

5. The descriptive approach and the OT. The tension between the meanings becomes further complicated when we turn to the nature of OT theology, and this for two main reasons: (a) The OT contains material from many centuries of Israelite life. This makes it obvious that there are different layers of meaning within the same account. The account of the sacrifice of Isaac may well once have functioned as God's own command of substituting an animal for human sacrifices, but in its present setting in Gen 22 the meaning is clearly seen as a witness to Abraham's ultimate obedience. Jacob's dream at Bethel seems to be a tradition by which the validity of the cult of the Northern kingdom was upheld by reference to how the patriarch had found Yahweh at that place, but once the rivalry between the two kingdoms was a dead issue, the story took on—or returned to—the meaning of a more general epiphany. This problem of interpretation and hermeneutics is certainly not confined to the OT; it forms the crucial problem of gospel research when we try to push beyond the evangelists to the actual words and deeds of Jesus. But in the OT it is a more flagrant and paramount problem. Thus already the descriptive task is faced with the constant question of "layers of meaning" through the history and transmission of OT traditions. The history of interpretation is woven into the very fabric of the biblical texts themselves, and the canonization of Torah, Prophets, and Writings did not disrupt the ongoing reinterpretation in sectarian or normative Judaism, as we learn from the intertestamental and the rabbinic material. Thus any statement of a descriptive sort about what an OT passage meant has to be accompanied by an address: for whom and at what stage of Israelite or Jewish history? The track along which the biblical theologian pursues the meaning of the OT is thus that of the ongoing religious life of Israel as the chosen people of God and as responding to the events in its history which they interpret as the acts of God.

(b) Second, the church was born out of a dispute with Jewish interpreters of the OT regarding its meaning, and first-century Christian theology of the more verbalized sort, as that found in Paul, centers around the terms on which the church finds the OT meaningful—e.g., as promise now fulfilled or as law binding on the members of the church. The Christian claim to the OT rested on the conviction that Jesus as the risen Christ was the Messiah to whom the OT witnessed. The church thereby sided with those interpreters of the OT who, like e.g., the Qumran community, saw the center of the OT in its prophecies and promises, including those found in the five books of the Law, while the Jewish exegesis which became normative more and more emphasized the commandments of the Torah as the core of revelation and the precious token of Israel's chosen status (*see* "Law in the OT" [in the *IDB*]). Neither interpretation had any similarity with the one prevailing in the theologized form of the Wellhausen interpretation of Israelite history, where the significance of the OT was seen in the evolution of ethical monotheism. Here, again, it was the radicals of the *religionsgeschichtliche Schule* who caused the construction of this liberal interpretation to crumble, corrupted and weakened as it was by the apologetic interest in a meaning for the present.

Any writer in the field of OT theology must be aware of this double outcome of the ongoing interpretation of the OT material, each within the framework of a community of faith. For the descriptive task both outcomes appear as live options, and neither of them can claim to be the right one if judged by the potentialities of the OT material itself. But the act of faith by which the interpretations parted ways does not add anything to the OT material as such. Thus a Christian and a Jewish OT theology differ only where the question of meaning is pursued beyond the material and the period of the OT texts themselves. Such a Christian OT theology may find its organizing principle in the NT understanding of the OT in first-century terms (another descriptive task being thus involved) or in any one principle of Christian hermeneutics from later centuries, our own included. Nobody could deny the validity or even the necessity for the church of such a task, especially since it is in the very tradition of the NT itself. Yet the same warning which emerged out of our study of the meanings in NT theology applies to such an enterprise. The distinction between the descriptive function as the core of all biblical theology on the one hand, and the hermeneutics and up-to-date translation on the other, must be upheld if there is to be any chance for the original to act creatively on the minds of theologians and believers of our time.

6. "Sacred history" and the unity of the Bible. In OT theology even more than its NT counterpart, history presents itself as the loom of the theological fabric. In spite of its intentions to be historical, the liberal interpretation of the OT overlooked this fact, substituting its evolutionistic interest in the development of ethics and monotheism for the sacred history in which Israel experienced its existence. In more recent times an anthropological approach to OT theology—not much different from Bultmann's approach, but unaware of its implicit demythologizing and dehistoricizing—has been tried with some success. Its success is partly due to its superior descriptive power if compared with that of the liberals.

In sharp contrast to what is called—with a gross generalization—"the Greek," we find the Semitic or Hebrew or biblical anthropology is hailed as the essence of biblical theology. But in works like those of G. E. Wright and G. von Rad, OT theology seeks its center where the ongoing life of Israel—from a descriptive point of view—experienced it—i.e., in its own history as a peculiar people, chosen by God. Especially in Wright this approach is coupled with arguments for the uniqueness of Israel as compared with surrounding people and cultures, a claim which seems to be a carry-over from another methodology. Israel's uniqueness was hardly based on its ideas about God or man but in its Election consciousness, which in turn has given its thinking distinctive features which we may well call unique (*see* "Covenant" [in the *IDB*]).

But the thrust of an OT theology which finds the canter in the acts of God (Wright) or in Yahweh's revelation through words and deeds in history (von Rad), is ultimately to establish that history is not only a stage upon which God (*see* "God, NT" [in the *IDB*]) displays his nature through his acts, but that the drama itself is one of history. The salvation which is promised is one within history, either in terms of return of the dispersed people from all the ends of the earth or as a New Jerusalem and a glorified Israel in a new age, which in spite of its otherworldly features comes in time and history at the end of this present age (*see* "Eschatology of the NT" [in the *IDB*]). This historical consciousness of Israel lives by the remembering of the past and the ever new interpretation of it as a promise for the future. The cultic festivals, with their roots in Near Eastern ritual and their manifestations in the sacred kingship of the Davidic dynasty, become projected toward the eschatological future of bliss, righteousness, and peace. In all this the common denominator—from a descriptive point of view—is neither certain concepts of God as One or as acting, nor an anthropology peculiar to the Bible, but the ongoing life of a people cultivating the traditions of its history in the light of its self-understanding. It is guided therein by its priests, prophets, and teachers of wisdom, and thus this people moves toward a sure but ever evasive eschaton, keeping the law, which is the token of their chosenness.

Such a framework for OT theology is the only one which takes the descriptive task seriously, since it does not borrow its categories from the NT or later Jewish or Christian interpretations but finds the organizing principle in the very life situations out of which the OT material emerges as meaningful to the life of the people. From such a layer of meaning we may move back into the meaning of the different elements which were placed in this framework of sacred history. This may lead us to patterns of thought and blocks of tradition originally quite unrelated to the historical consciousness of Israel; but only with a full recognition of the framework can we adequately go behind it and analyze what the original elements of the tradition may have been and how they were modified by their setting in the religion of Israel. Only so can we know to what extent they retained their character as remnants—whether weak or vigorous and creative—of an earlier period within the total tradition. As such remnants they deserve the fullest descriptive treatment and should not be swallowed up by a generalizing sweep of sacred history as though that sweep constituted the entire content of the OT.

When the OT is treated in this fashion as the living and

growing tradition of a people, it yields a theology which brings us up to the parting of the ways by Jews and Christians. The description thereof places us where the NT stands, and we face the issues of NT theology as once Jews and Christians faced them in the first century. It brings into the NT the dimension of time and history which is essential to our understanding of the NT in its own terms. The announcement by Jesus that the new age is impending, and the faith of the early church that the Messiah is enthroned in heaven since he is risen and since the Holy Spirit has been poured out, come as vigorous claims for fulfilment of the OT promises, not accepted by the majority of the Jews. Yet Paul is convinced that before the kingdom is established on earth as it is now in heaven, the Jews will accept Jesus as the Messiah (Rom 9–11). Thereby the drama of this age will come to its glorious end; the new age will be ushered in. Jewish exegesis in the Christian era went rather in another direction, and the eschatology which had reached its peak in Christianity as well as in parts of Judaism became more and more toned down. The emphasis shifted from the hopes for the future to the obedience in the present under the law. Rabbinic Judaism established itself as the normative interpretation of the OT, but the common denominator remained the same: the Election consciousness which accepts the law as the gracious token of God's special favor to his people.

The only question which is beyond reach for such a descriptive approach is: Who was right—the Jews or the Christians? Its answer remains what it always was, an act of faith. If we approached OT theology in terms of developing ethical monotheism, we could, at least theoretically, arrive at an answer. This is , at any rate, what the liberal theologians implied when they hailed Jesus as a teacher superior both to the best of the prophets and to the wisest of the rabbis. But once we have accepted history as the fabric of biblical theology, we are thrown back to the same choice of faith which faced the first century. History does not answer such questions; it only poses them.

This highly simplified sketch of biblical theology in the encounter between the testaments suggests also in what sense there can be a biblical theology where the OT and the NT are held together as a unity. The significance of the OT for the NT is thus shown to be inescapable, just as it was in the early church before there was a NT in our sense. On the basis of the OT and its fulfilment in Christ rests the Christian claim to be the chosen ones of God, the true Israel in Christ, and—if Gentile by birth—"honorary Jews," heirs to the promises given to Israel. The crucial question arises when we ask what impact the NT should have on the presentation of OT theology. When biblical theology allows for such impact, it goes beyond its descriptive task, unless what is being attempted is merely a description of how the early church understood the unity between the OT and its fulfilment in what came to be the NT. But if the biblical theologian should go on to say that this is consequently what the OT text means, he would be making either a statement of his own faith or a statement about the faith of the NT. If he says that this is what the OT means for the present day Christian, he has proceeded from description via hermeneutics, to a contemporary interpretation.

Thus the treatment of the Bible as a unity in this sense is beyond the task of descriptive biblical theology. Indeed, such a biblical theology will tend to discourage and prevent too facile a unification. To cite one example: Paul's radical concentration on the OT promises and his view of the law as holy and yet obsolete, once Christ has come, led Marcion to do away with the OT. He was in a certain way faithful to Paul—far more so than some Jewish Christians—but since his conceptual framework did not allow for a god who dealt with mankind differently in different dispensations, he could not imagine God as the originator of a holy law which he later declared obsolete. In its defense against Marcion, the church by and large forgot Paul's dialectic of time, and leaned over backward placing the OT and the NT on an equal basis. A truly descriptive biblical theology would have prevented both extremes. Thus the historian, with his descriptive approach, may clarify the issue of the relation between the two testaments.

There is, however, one way in which descriptive biblical

theology does consider the Bible as a unity. The "sacred history" continues into the NT. Israel's election consciousness is transferred and heightened by the Christians—Jews and Gentiles alike. History is still the matrix of theology. Jesus does not come with a new doctrine about forgiveness for sinners; when he comes, "it so happens" that sinners accept him and the righteous do not. The first shall be the last. He does not leave his disciples primarily as a group of pupils who have rehearsed the "teachings of Jesus" as a lesson to teach others, but he has promised them a place as princes in the new Israel and has urged them to watch for the signs of the times and the coming of the kingdom. They do so; and his Resurrection and the Holy Spirit are indications to them that Jesus is now enthroned as the Christ on the right hand of God. The Parousia must be close at hand, and the Spirit is the efficient and sufficient down payment of their share in the age to come. As Israel lives through its history as a chosen people, so are the Christians now gathered together as the chosen ones, the church enjoying a higher degree of anticipation of God's redeeming grace and power than did even the messianic sect at Qumran. God is still the God of a people with an ongoing history, however short it may be: the NT develops its ecclesiology.

It is in such a framework that NT theology can be properly described, and this framework is basically the same as that of OT theology. Here is the common denominator from a descriptive point of view. Within this framework, which gives us the *Sitz im Leben* of NT thought as a message and a self-presentation, we may study different ideas and concepts. We may find out how they are related or how they conflict with one another. But none of these ideas exists as general and eternal truth apart from the self-understanding of the church as the chosen community.

Thus there is a unity of the Bible on a historical basis. And this is the basis on which the two testaments came together. If, on the other hand, we approach the unity of the Bible or one of the testaments from the point of view of concepts and ideas, we may still be able to discern a certain unity in its anthropology, in its concept of God, or in its attitude toward ethics. A descriptive study of, e.g., Paul's concept of justification would find the roots in the Song of Deborah, perhaps the oldest piece of tradition in the whole Bible (Judg 5:11; צדקות = "saving acts of God"). The Gospel of Mark could be seen in relation to the kerygma in Acts 10 and 1 Cor 15, as we have learned from C. H. Dodd's *Apostolic Preaching and Its Developments*. But we would look for a type of unity which was different from the organic unity to which the testaments themselves witness. And we would be faced with a diversity of views without the means to understand how they fell into a meaningful pattern for the biblical writers themselves. Paul's dialectic attitude toward the law—mentioned above in comparison with Marcion—is a case in point. We would be inclined to see a great—or merely contradictory—paradox in his statement about the holiness and the obsoleteness of the law, if we did not recognize that Paul thought in the pattern of dispensations. The tension between the teaching of Jesus and the early theology of the church would remain a total enigma were it not for the fact that the disciples interpreted what followed after his death as a drastic step forward in the timetable of God, leading toward the Parousia. Our Description has to detect and clarify such a development. It could, however, hardly answer the question whether the disciples were right or wrong in their interpretation. We can only describe what they did and why they thought they were right while others thought they were wrong.

What has now been presented as the first and crucial task of biblical theology—i.e., its descriptive function—thus yields the original in its own terms, limiting the interpretation to what it meant in its own setting. An attempt has been made to show that such a task does not necessarily imply the disintegration of the biblical material into unrelated bits of antiquated information. It is quite capable of presenting the different elements as an organic unity *if that unity is the one which actually holds the material together in the Bible itself.* It has been indicated that any question of meaning beyond the one suggested by the sources themselves tends to lessen the challenge of the original to the

present-day theologian and makes him unaware of the hermeneutic problem as a *sine qua non* for any such interpretation.

B. The Hermeneutic Question

1. As raised by a descriptive biblical theology. A more thor-
ough familiarity with the net result of such a descriptive approach as the one outlined above raises the hermeneutic
question in a somewhat new form. No period of Christian theology has been as radically exposed to a consistent attempt to re-
live the theology of its first adherents. The ideal of an empathetic
understanding of the first century without borrowing categories from later times has never been an ideal before, not have the
comparative sources for such an adventure been as close at hand
and as well analyzed. There have always been bits and pieces of
an appeal to the original meaning over against different later
dogmas and practices of the church. The School of Antioch
fought the School of Alexandria by such means; the Reformers
argued with the papal theologians, and the Anabaptists with the
Reformers, on such a basis; the pietists criticized the orthodox
scholastics in the same fashion, and the liberal theologians
claimed the same type of arguments against the evangelicals,
etc. But never before was there a frontal nonpragmatic,
nonapologetic attempt to describe OT or NT faith and practice
from within its original presuppositions, and with due attention
to its own organizing principles, regardless of its possible ramifications for those who live by the Bible as the Word of God.

The descriptive approach has led us far beyond a conglom-
eration of diverse ideas, the development of which we may be
able to trace. We are now ushered right into a world of biblical
thought which deserves the name "theology" just as much as
do the thoughts of Augustine, Thomas, Calvin, and Schleiermacher. The translation of its content cannot any more be
made piecemeal. The relation to the historical record is not any
more one where systematic theology takes the raw material of
nonsystematic data of revelation and gives to it systematic
structure and theological stature. The relation is not one be-

tween a witness of a theologically innocent faith and a mature and sophisticated systematic theology. It is a relation between two highly developed types of theology. On the one hand, theologies of history, from which all statements about God, Christ, man, righteousness, and salvation derive their meaning and connotations, in terms of their function within the plan and on the plane of history; and on the other hand, theologies of an ontological sort, where Christianity is understood in terms of the nature of God, Christ, man, etc. (*see* "God, NT"; "Christ"; "Man, Nature of (NT)" [all in the *IDB*]).

Within this pattern of nature or essence Christian theology has always tried to do justice to the historical element in the biblical material. But under the pressure of the thought-pattern inherent in the Western theological approach, biblical eschatology—i.e., the matrix of NT thought—was taken care of in a "last chapter" of systematic theology dealing with the "last things" (*see* "Eschatology of the NT" [in the *IDB*]). Thereby the very structure of biblical thought was transformed and its eschatology inactivated.

In more recent Protestant theology there have been serious attempts to do more justice to eschatology as the overarching category of systematic theology and the motif of the "two aeons," this age and the age to come, has been stressed—e.g., by the Lundensian theologians. But once again the outcome is a radical transformation, in that the aeons become internalized as levels of existence and experience in the mind and life of every Christian according to the formula "at the same time justified and sinner." The life on the border between the two dispensations as Paul knew them is lifted out of its historical context and becomes a timeless description of an inner dialectic of the Christian existence.

The focal point for a theological preservation of the historical dimension in the biblical material was found quite naturally in the stern insistence on the Incarnation in Jesus Christ. But in this process the Incarnation was more and more intensively developed in terms of its ramifications for the nature of Jesus Christ, while its original connotations were far more centered in the chronological pattern of the Johannine Prologue: God has *now* come to men in Jesus Christ to tabernacle among them in a glory which outshone that of Moses and the law.

The situation could perhaps be best analyzed in the realm of NT Christology (*see* "Christ" [in the *IDB*]), where significant strands of tradition display what later on came to be branded and banned as adoptionism—i.e., the concept of Jesus, who was made the Christ in his Baptism, or in his Resurrection, or by his Ascension [*see* those articles in the *IDB*]. In the light of later doctrinal development it is easy to see why such a Christology was deemed heretical. But there is no indication that there was any conscious tension or argument, within the NT and in its time, between an adoptionist position and one which spoke of Jesus Christ in terms of pre-existence or virgin birth. This was apparently not a matter of conflict. It became so only when the biblical witness was forced to yield the answer to the question about the nature of Jesus Christ, and when this very question became the shibboleth of true doctrine. As long as the question remains within the theology of history, it does not ask what Jesus Christ is or how human and divine nature go together in him. It centers around the question: Who is he? Is he the Messiah or isn't he? In such a context an adoptionist answer coincides for all practical purposes with that of the pre-existence type. But once this framework is lost, the answers come miles apart from one another as contradictory, and the kerygmatic statements in Acts 2:32–37 are a sheer liability to the orthodox theologian when they hail Jesus as the one whom God has made both Lord and Christ after his crucifixion, placing him on his right side as the enthroned Messiah in heaven, whence he now could and did pour out the promised Holy Spirit as a sizable down payment of the age to come.

It is perhaps even more striking when Acts 3:18–21 urges repentance in order that times of refreshment might come from God and that he might send the aforetime-appointed Messiah, namely Jesus, who is now retained in heaven. Here the Parousia is really not the Second Coming of later theology. There is only one coming of the Messiah, the one at the end of time. We are used to considering the First Coming—i.e., the earthly ministry of Jesus, as a clear, uncomplicated "coming" of the Messiah, but recognize how many complications arose out of the interpretation of the Second Coming. To the theology manifested in Acts 3, the problem seems to have been the opposite one. The Parousia—what we call the Second Coming—was no "problem"; it was part of the Jewish expectations concerning the age to come. The problem was rather in the opposite direction: To what extent was the First Coming, the earthly ministry of Jesus, a real coming? How much of an anticipation did it imply, and to what extent did Jesus exercise messianic power within it? Once he was hailed as the Messiah enthroned in heaven, it was clear to the gospel writers that Jesus was the Christ, but there are enough indications left in the Synoptic gospels to show that he was so by inference from what had happened after Calvary, and by references about what he was to become.

Thus the pattern of history in this type of NT theology sheds new light on the discussion about the messianic consciousness of Jesus. Those who deny such a consciousness and credit the church with having made Jesus their Messiah overlook the nature of this theology of history, for which there needed to be no distortion of facts in the belief that Jesus was made the Messiah in his ascension and enthronement. Those who claim a straight messianic consciousness in Jesus overlook the evidence that the messiahship in Jesus' earthly ministry has a strong futuristic note. But from the vantage point of post-Resurrection/Ascension the church confesses: Jesus is the Messiah now, and consequently he was the Messiah then—but he had not really become so by then, nor is he yet the Messiah here on earth as he is to be at the Parousia. Such an attempt to catch the theological meaning as found in Acts 2–3 gives no sense to one who inquires into the nature of Jesus Christ, and it sounds strange to any "yes-or-no" approach to the problem of the messianic consciousness of Jesus. But it was highly significant to those who were eager to understand where they were in the messianic timetable of Jewish and Christian eschatology.

He who changes the question can only be misled or confused by using the biblical text as a direct answer to it.

Texts and problems have been chosen from some of the highly controversial areas of NT exegesis only as illustrations to clarify the problem before us. The exegesis involved may well require correction or refutation, but the thrust of the descriptive method would always be of the same nature. The hermeneutic problem of biblical theology therefore centers in the clash between two types of theology. Each type includes a wide variety of alternatives. On the biblical side there are the different types of OT theology, some contemporary with one another, some later developments of earlier strata. In the NT it is somewhat easier to discern a Matthean, Markan, Lukan, Johannine, or Pauline theology, etc. But they all live within the presupposition of their respective centuries, and they all answer questions which require a historical consciousness and an awareness of where in God's history they now stand.

On the systematic side there is perhaps an even greater diversity, but in our Western tradition we find questions asked by the systematic theologian to be by their very nature above history and beyond change. Such a systematic approach has been considerably intensified by biblical criticism, with its radical doubt or mild uncertainty about many events and data on which systematic theology would have to rest its case. Lessing's statement that eternal truth cannot be derived from historical data became the more pertinent to systematic theology once the biblical basis for orthodox Christianity was summoned to constant trial before the courts of historical criticism. But in a certain sense Christian theology had freed itself from its historical matrix already in the time of the apologists of the second century when the case for Christianity was spelled out in the terms of Hellenistic philosophy. It would be unwise to exclude some elements within the OT and the NT from a similar tendency; thus the need for and the possibility of a translation of biblical theology into new categories of thought is taken for granted from the very outset. Orthodoxy never had repristination as its program in the periods of its strength. The possibility of translation was given—as it is for Barth—in the reality of the subject matter, apart from its intellectual manifestation in the thought-patterns of the original documents. God and Christ were not Semites in such a sense that the biblical pattern of thought was identified with revelation itself.

Consequently, theology through the centuries acted in great freedom and with good conscience and considerable creativity. The fathers and the Reformers alike had no idea of a biblical theology apart from other theological endeavors. They were convinced that they were biblical theologians in the only sense one could be a theologian; in this respect Barth is certainly right in claiming the authority of Calvin and Luther for his biblical approach. But once the concern for a biblical theology as distinguished from other types of systematic theology has made itself manifest, a new problem arises. By way of a wide variety of hybrids where systematic and biblical categories were hopelessly intermingled, this concern has now brought us to the point where we can make reasonably clear statements about the meanings of the original in its own terms. This is why we have the right to say that the result of descriptive biblical theology has raised the hermeneutic problem in a somewhat new form.

2. Alternative answers to the hermeneutic question. In the light of descriptive biblical theology, it becomes possible to pass tentative and relative judgments on the alternative ways in which systematic theologians have stated the meaning for the present day—or for all times, if that is their conscious aim—of the biblical material. Such judgments can be made on the basis of the degree to which systematic theology succeeds in communicating the intention implied in the biblical texts, an intention which only a precise and un-compromised study of the original could detect. But such a judgment would always remain tentative, since the task of systematic theology is by its very nature one of translation from one pattern of thought into another, and every true and great translation is a creative effort, not just a painstaking and nearsighted exchange of the precise words of one language with its lexicographical equivalents in another language. Aquila's Greek text stands as the horrifying example of such a senseless approach. On the linguistic level we hold the view—at least Protestants do—that there is no language into which the Bible could not be translated well enough to communicate its message; and the student of the Greek gospels is already once removed from the Aramaic vernacular of Jesus' teaching. If this analogy were one of considerable precision, it would imply that there could be few philosophies, epistemologies, anthropologies, etc., which could not furnish the framework for a systematic theology by which the meaning of the Christian scripture could be stated. The history of Christian theology gives us reason to accept the analogy to a considerable extent. And the fact that the original is available gives us the right and the audacity to encourage such translation activity.

The attempt of the so-called liberal theology to detect the meaning for today in the evolution of an even more refined religious insight with a higher level of ethics could hardly be ruled out as one of the alternative answers to the quest for meaning. Its validity as a Christian theology would hinge upon its ability to live with a growing awareness that its categories of meaning are utterly alien to biblical thought. Such an awareness is harder for the liberals to take than for any other theologians, since they traditionally have rested their case on its historical truth, and claimed the historical Jesus as the first protagonist for their own views. In their attempt to grasp the intention of the biblical message, they were unusually handicapped.

In the wake of liberal theology in its academic form—in its popular form it is still very much with us—came the tendency to establish contact with the world of descriptive biblical theology by simply substituting its categories for those traditional to Western theology. Well aware of the peril of modernizing Jesus, one was less afraid of archaizing oneself. The achievements of the descriptive biblical theology were dumped right into the twentieth century. The fact that those results now displayed enough structure and religious intensity to give the impression of a real theology made it quite tempting to try such a return to the prelogical, the Semitic, the Hebraic, the first century. All these categories were now subsumed under the heading "biblical" and this in an evaluating fashion, so that the theological ideal became an ill-considered parallel to the well-considered descriptive ideal of divesting oneself of the twentieth century. The "biblical way of thinking" was spelled out over against "the Greek." Once more the descriptive and the contemporary became interwoven, this time on the terms of the result of the descriptive approach. From a theological point of view this meant that revelation was identified with patterns of thought and culture; the need or the possibility of creative translation—i.e., the very glory of systematic theology through the ages—was undercut. No serious attempts at a conscious translation were made.

Such criticism could certainly not be directed against what we may call the thoroughgoing translations, where the tendency is ahistorical or even antihistorical. Paul Tillich and Rudolf Bultmann are two pronounced representatives of such answers to the hermeneutic problem. Neither of them finds anything normative in a theology of history as presented by the descriptive approach. To both of them history is utterly mute as far as theological meaning is concerned. Secondly, historical data are to them too shaky a foundation for the theological enterprise. Tillich thus approaches theology from an analysis of Being, and he is consistent enough to claim no, or little, biblical support for such a category. Bultmann, on the other hand, finds his point of departure as well as arrival in human self-understanding, and for this he claims considerable biblical authority, since according to him, the very intention of the kerygma (see "Preaching" [in the *IDB*]) is to challenge man's self-understanding. It appears, however, that Tillich, in spite of being perhaps the least "biblical"—in a conscious sense and by mode of language—of all contemporary theologians, is capable of communicating a wider range of biblical intention than does Bultmann with his highly anthropological concentration.

The most common response to the challenge of descriptive biblical theology is perhaps what may be called the semi-historical translation. Here the historical nature of revelation is taken seriously. The Bible is the record of the acts of God in history, and the kerygma is the powerful proclamation of these acts, a proclamation which shares in the creative power of the acts themselves. Thus the church is nurtured and renewed through the ages by this creative Word by which it rehearses the acts of God in sacred history. But somewhere along the line this scared history has stopped, and there is only plain history left, with a more general Providence at work. Thereby the God who acts becomes more and more the God who did act in biblical history. Consequently his acts appear as performed on the stage of history in order to demonstrate his nature. Theology reads his nature off the record of sacred history. The acts of God in history and the human response to them become calcified into a mold. This mold is then used by theology to make the true images or concepts of God as "He Who Acts." The difficulty with such a translation into non-propositional and non-philosophical concepts is that it accepts the historical framework of biblical thought for biblical times, since it yields the illustrations for our grasp of God's nature and will; but once the canon of the NT has drawn the line, there is a change of categories. Sacred history has come to an end, and what remains is a history where these deep-frozen images of God's acts are constantly brought to life in the remembrance of the church. The tension between a historical understanding of the Bible and a theologically void history of the church raises grave problems of inconsistency.

Such a problem would lead us to suggest that the only consistent alternatives would be either a radical, ahistorical translation as mentioned above, or—if the historical framework of biblical thought were to be retained—a systematic theology where the bridge between the centuries of biblical events and our own time was found in the actual history of the church as still ongoing sacred history of God's people. The blueprint for such a theology could be found in that self-understanding of Israel, both new and old, which descriptive biblical theology has laid bare as the common denominator of biblical thought. Such a theology would conceive of the Christian existence as a life by the fruits of God's acts in Jesus Christ, rather than as a faith according to concepts deduced from the teaching of the prophets, Jesus, and Paul regarding God's acts. It would exercise some of the same freedom which Paul's and the other NT letters do when they refrain from any nostalgic attempts to play Galilee into their theology by transforming the teaching of Jesus' earthly ministry into a system of theology and ethics. It would recognize that God is still the God who acts in history when he leads his church to new lands and new cultures and new areas of concern. A theology which retains history as a theologically charged category finds in its ecclesiology the overarching principles of interpretation and meaning. It does not permit its ecclesiology to be transferred to the second last chapter in its systematic works, followed by that on an equally inactivated eschatology. A theological awareness of sacred history seems to imply by inner necessity a growing recognition of the church as something far beyond an organization for the promotion of evangelism and theology. Through the ongoing sacred history, which is commonly labeled "church history," the fruits of God's acts in covenant and in the Christ are handed down to the present time. Within this history the task of preaching and theology under the guidance of the Holy Spirit is part of an ongoing sacred history. The chasm between the centuries is theologically as well as historically bridged by history itself, not only by a timeless kerygma which reaches the individual in ever-repeated punctiliar action. The church lives, not only by the aorist of the Holy Spirit, but by the perfect tense as the Greeks understood it: an action which is completed and the effects of which are still with us.

3. The significance of "canon" for biblical theology. Such an approach would raise the question of the canon (i.e., the limitation of the Bible to—usually—sixty-six books, thirty-nine in the OT and twenty-seven in the NT) in its sharpest form [*see* "Canon" in the *IDB*]. As far as the descriptive approach goes, the canon can have no crucial significance. The church has a "Bible," but descriptive approach knows it only as the "Bible of the church." In order to grasp the meaning of an OT or NT text in its own time, the comparative material—e.g., the intertestamental literature (Enoch, Testaments of the Twelve Patriarchs, Jubilees, etc.; *see* Apocrypha; Pseudepigrapha [in the *IDB*]) or the Apostolic Fathers, some of which clearly antedate some NT writings—is of equal or even greater significance than some canonical material. The revival of biblical theology in our own generation depends greatly on the way in which such material was brought to bear on the original meaning of biblical texts. But when the descriptive task is addressing itself to the interplay between different parts of the Bible, as e.g., the NT understanding of the OT, it naturally takes cognizance of the limits of, as well as of the very idea of, canon. The descriptive approach also yields considerable insight into the nature and motivations for canonization itself and is capable of understanding the need as well as the rationalization connected with the long process of canonization. This in itself is one of the most puzzling and fascinating interplays of historical circumstances and theological concerns.

Once we go beyond the descriptive approach, the canon of scripture becomes crucial. To many of the modern types of biblical theology, the phenomenon of canonical scriptures seems to count little. To Barth it is inspiration [*see* "Inspiration" in the *IDB*] rather than canon that matters, and the process of canonization is an external feature which neither adds to nor subtracts from the power of the inspired writings to allow the Word to authenticate itself ever anew to him who hears. This is actually consistent with an ahistorical theology, since canonization so obviously is a historical process. It strikes the historian, nevertheless, that the concept of inspiration was of little or no avail in the first centuries of church history, when the church moved toward a closed canon. Apostolic origin, a doctrine in agreement with the succession of teaching, and wide usage and recognition in the churches were the chief criteria when the early church dealt with a wide range of writings of which many were recognized as equally inspired with those finally received among the twenty-seven. But once the canon was closed, the doctrine of inspiration served well as an answer to the question: Why are these books different from all other books? To Bultmann, canon seems to be of little significance. The Christian self-understanding, to which the Bible caters, is found within it, but there are also parts of it which do not display it. Furthermore, its meaning for the present rests on the same basis as that on which any historical document has "meaning" beyond its value as a source for historical information. Finally, the understanding of the intention of the Bible as kerygmatic is not deduced from its canonical nature; on the contrary, it is the kerygmatic nature which gives the Bible its claim to authority.

To the radically historical alternative, as outlined above, much depends on the understanding of canon as a crucial category of any theological enterprise. This is certainly what we would expect if the historical nature of revelation is retained in a theologically potent framework of the sacred history of God's people. It is quite significant that, e.g., a biblical theologian like Cullmann, who has given such a strong impetus to the historical alternative, has also addressed himself extensively to the problem of *tradition* and canonization (*see* the chapters "The Plurality of the Gospels as a Theological Problem in Antiquity" and "The Tradition," in *The Early Church* [1956]), and that his discussion takes the form of a new attempt to clarify how Protestant and Roman Catholic theology differ in their understanding of the interplay between the continuous tradition and the line drawn around the Bible by canonization.

To the historical approach the question raised by Harnack's studies in the NT canon becomes theologically significant: Why is there a NT, not only a fourth part added to the three units of the OT (Law, Prophets, Writings)? The descriptive approach suggests a theological answer: The NT—as well as the church itself—rests on the return of the Spirit. Judaism in the time of Jesus lived under the conviction that the Spirit had ceased, and when the question of valid scriptures was discussed, this cessation was related to the last of the prophets (i.e., Malachi). They recognized themselves as living in a period when Israel depended on the scriptural interpretations of scribes whose authority rested on faithful transmission, not on the Spirit in which one could say, as the prophets had done, "Thus saith the Lord." But they cherished the hope and the promise of the return of the Spirit. This would be one of the crucial manifestations of the coming of the new age. Thus it is quite natural that the conviction of the church that this new age had arrived and manifested itself in the Holy Spirit also gave the basis and theological rationale for what came to be the NT.

It is worth noting, however, that the closing of the NT canon is not based on any argument similar to that of Judaism regarding the OT—viz., that the Spirit ceased again. Such a view would have undercut the very faith and life of the church and was never considered in the argumentation regarding the NT canon in the first centuries. The development from diversified oral and written traditions to the twenty-seven books of the NT was of a more historical nature, guided by the necessity to protect the original from more and more undependable elaborations and distortions, some "heretical" but quite a few properly orthodox in their intentions. The gift of prophetic and inspired teaching was still a recognized phenomenon, an ever-repeated "aorist" of God's dealing with his church. But the significance of Jesus Christ and his apostles as ἐφάπαξ ("once for all"), and as the very basis on which the church was built—i.e., the "perfect-tense" dimension of biblical thought, as referred to above—called for a distinction between this and what the church understood as original and as its magna charta. Thus Cullmann seems to be right when he suggests that early Christian tradition bore within it the element which served as a compelling cause for the process of canonization. This element may be defined as the "perfect-tense" element of Christian theology. As such it affirms the acts of God as unique in Christ and his apostles, but it also points toward an ongoing history of the theological existence of the church. God's acts are not punctiliar aorists, frozen and canned within the canon, nor do they belong to the timeless present tense of mysticism.

The question as to the meaning of the Bible in the present— as distinguished from the meaning in the past as stated by descriptive biblical theology—receives its theological answer from the canonical status of scripture. In its most radical form, the question was: Do these old writings have any meaning beyond their significance as sources for the past? On what basis could it be valid to translate them into new modes of thought? On what basis could such an original—and such a translation—have a normative function for the life of the church? Such questions can be answered only within the consciousness of the church. The answer rests on the act of faith by which Israel and its sister by adoption, the church, recognizes its history as sacred history, and finds in these writings the epitome of the acts of God. As such these writings are meaningful to the church in any age. It is as canon, and only as canon, that there is a Bible, an OT and a NT as well as the whole Bible of the church as a unity. The old question of wether the Bible rests on the church or the church on the Bible is a misleading question from the point of view of the historical alternative. To be sure, the church "chose" its canon. But it did so under the impact of the acts of God by which it itself came into existence. The process of canonization is one of recognition, not one of creation *ex nihilo* or *ex theologia*.

One could perhaps see the Protestant Reformation as a reaffirmation of the line drawn protectively around the canon. In a situation when the growth of tradition threatened to submerge the "original"—as had the traditions rejected as non-canonical in the second and third centuries—Luther and Calvin reinforce the distinctiveness of the original and its superior authority in the life of the church. There are many things which we would like to know, historically as well as theologically, beyond what the Scriptures tell us. In the Roman Catholic tradition such quite legitimate and pious curiosity has centered around Mary, the mother of Jesus. Against such and other elaborating traditions the Reformers take a firm stand on *sola scriptura* as sufficient, yea, more than sufficient, unto salvation. The canon is enforced, and such a return to the "original"— given the circumstances of the time—engenders one of the most spectacular renewals of theology and church life that history has seen.

This is in its own way a suggestive illustration of how an exposure to the "original" plays into the life of the church. It gives us theology in a new key and breaks through many cherished presuppositions. It is perhaps not too much to suggest that the highly developed descriptive biblical theology of our own period in the long run may have a similar effect. This is not to hail our age as capable of a new Reformation. But it does suggest that all theological renewal and creativity has as one of its components a strong exposure to the "original" beyond the presuppositions and the inherited frame of thought of our immediate predecessors in the theological task. Otherwise the history of theology would be an uninterrupted chain reaction of a philosophical nature, with Augustine correcting the earlier fathers, Thomas Aquinas correcting Augustine, Luther refuting Thomas, Schleiermacher touching up Luther and Barth, and Tillich carrying the traditional discussion up to our own time. The exposure to the "original" as it is made accessible by descriptive biblical theology, could give an alternative to such a development. This alternative is not new in principle; it has been at work through the ages. What is new is the radical concern for the original *in its own terms.*

If we were to take an extreme example of what this could imply, we could return to the area of Christology. We saw how in the NT "adoptionism" stands as an equal, side by side with other types of Christology, and how the reasons for its downfall were found, not in the NT, but in the framework of later philosophical presuppositions. If the ontology which caused its downfall in the theology of the church were not any more a live option to the philosophical structure of a systematic theology of our time, it would be quite possible to speak meaningfully and in a most orthodox manner about Christ in "adoptionist" terms when witnessing to his function and his reality. There may be many and other reasons why this specific case should not be followed up; our only concern is to indicate in what way a descriptive biblical theology gives the systematic theologian a live option to attempt a direct translation of the biblical material, not a revision of a translation of a revision of a translation. . . . It is easy to see the great need for such a possibility in the theology on the mission field and in the young churches, and there are signs that Western Christianity could be well served by a similar approach, with its sharp distinction between past and present meaning.

4. The preacher and biblical theology. A sharp distinction between what the texts meant in their original setting and what they mean in the present has considerable ramification for the work of the preacher, if he in any sense sees it as his task to communicate the message of the Bible to the congregation whose shepherd he is, and to the world which is his mission field. If we may use once more the analogy of the original and the translation—and this should not be considered more than an approximate analogy—the preacher is called upon to function as the bilingual translator. He should through his training and his ongoing studies attain the marks of a truly bilingual person—i.e., one who is capable of thinking in two languages. (By "languages" are meant, not the Greek and Hebrew of the Bible—although these would become more and more indispensable if the "bilingual" approach were taken seriously—but the modes and patterns of thought in the Bible.) His familiarity with the biblical world and patterns of thought should, through his work in descriptive biblical theology, have reached the point where he is capable of moving around in his Bible with idiomatic ease. His familiarity with the "language" of the contemporary world should reach a similar degree of perception and genuine understanding. Only so could he avoid the rhetorical truisms of much homiletic activity, where the message is expressed in a strange—sometimes even beautiful—mixed tongue, a homiletical Yiddish which cannot be really understood outside the walls of the Christian ghetto.

The demand for such a bilingual function of the preaching ministry may seem quite exacting, and indeed it is. It is also as it should be that the work of biblical as well as systematic theology finds its functional focus in the pulpit of the church. But it would be unreasonable to demand of the preacher—if now we may press our analogy once more—to become an academic grammarian of these two "languages" or a master of philosophical semantics. His task and his competence would remain by and large on the level of the vernacular, which he should have overheard long enough to be able to use it naturally and easily, as he would also use the Bible.

A mere repetition and affirmation of the biblical language, or even a translation which mechanically substitutes contemporary terms—often with a psychological slant—for those of the original, has little chance to communicate the true intention of the biblical text. To use an example from Bultmann's demand for demythologizing, the mere statement "Jesus is risen" directs the mind of most listeners toward a unique phenomenon, glorious or impossible as the case may be. On the basis of this phenomenon the believer is invited to base his hope for eternal life. A closer descriptive study of the resurrection passages suggests, however, that to the first listeners to the kerygma the phenomenon of the Resurrection was not surprising in the same sense. All Jews—except the Sadducees—expected the Resurrection as the climax of God's history; the phenomenon was nothing strange and new to them. The only new thing was that it had happened. The claim of the church that Jesus was risen thus meant to those who accepted it that the general resurrection, to which they looked forward, had started to happen; Paul consequently says that Christ has been raised as the "first fruits of those who have fallen asleep" (1 Cor. 15:20). In the same chapter the argument runs partly in the opposite direction to what we are used to think: "If there is no general resurrection, then Christ has not been raised" (v. 13; cf. v. 16). Those who first heard and believed the news about the Resurrection were not absorbed in a consideration of the phenomenon as such, but received it as a message that the new age had started to manifest itself here and now. This certainly affirmed their hopes in sharing in Christ's resurrection in God's good time, but the center of the message was that the power of the new age was at work in their own world and their own time.

Bultmann suggests that the task of the preacher is to free this message from its biblical nucleus, the proclaimed fact of the Resurrection as a historical event. But even for a preacher, who finds reason to object to such a demythologizing or dehistoricizing of the gospel, the problem which Bultmann points up remains a real one. Can the preacher say that he has communicated the message of Easter by stating and by underscoring the physical nature of the phenomenon of the Resurrection as a stumbling block for unbelievers, but a rock of salvation for those who believe? His familiarity with the results of a descriptive biblical theology would urge him to place the emphasis where the texts themselves put it and to meditate, e.g., along the lines of how the power of the new age manifested itself in Jesus Christ, not only as a token of our resurrection, but as the enthronement of Christ and as the possibility for man to live by the powers of the new age here and now. There would be many other lines like this which opened up from the gospel of Easter if the preacher did not become paralyzed—in faith or in doubts—by the phenomenon of the Resurrection, deducing from it theological propositions, but let his familiarity with the biblical world guide him through the concrete and diversified way in which the early church recognized and rejoiced in the resurrection of Jesus Christ. His homiletic imagination would become enriched, and the message would have a chance to find live and relevant translation.

If the pulpit is—as suggested here—the true *Sitz im Leben*, "life situation," where meaning of the original meets with the meanings for today, then it is once more clear that we cannot pursue the study of biblical theology adequately if the two tenses are not kept apart. For the descriptive biblical theologian this is a necessity implied in his own discipline; and whether he is a believer or an agnostic, he demands respect for the descriptive task as an enterprise valid in its own right and for its own sake. For the life of the church such a consistent descriptive approach is a great and promising asset which enables the church, its teaching and preaching ministry, to be exposed to the Bible in its original intention and intensity, as an ever new challenge to thought, faith, and response.

Appendix 2

The Ethics of Biblical Interpretation: Decentering Biblical Scholarship

Elisabeth Schüssler Fiorenza

[Note: This is the text of the Society of Biblical Literature Presidential Address delivered 5 December 1987 at the SBL Annual Meeting held at the Copley Marriott Hotel, Boston, MA. It is reprinted here from *JBL* 107 (1988): 3–17.]

It is commonplace that presidential addresses have primarily rhetorical functions. They are a ceremonial form of speech that does not invite responsive questions nor questioning responses. Such presidential rhetoric is generally of two sorts: either it addresses a particular exegetical, archaeological, or historical problem, or it seeks to reflect on the status of the field by raising organizational, hermeneutical, or methodological questions. The latter type sometimes attempts to chart the paradigm shifts or decentering processes in biblical scholarship which displace the dominant ethos of research but do not completely replace it or make it obsolete.

Almost eighty years ago, in his presidential address entitled "The Bearing of Historical Studies on the Religious Use of the Bible," Frank Porter of Yale University charted three such shifts: (1) The first stage, out of which biblical scholarship had just emerged, was the stage in which the book's records are imposed upon the present as an external authority. (2) The second stage, through which biblical scholarship was passing in 1908, was that of historical science, which brings deliverance from dogmatic bondage and teaches us to view the past as past, biblical history like other histories, and the Bible like other books.

(3) Porter envisioned a third stage "at which, while the rights and achievements of historical criticism are freely accepted, the power that lives in the book is once more felt."[1] He likens this third stage to the reading of great books, whose greatness does not consist in their accuracy as records of facts, but depends chiefly on their symbolic power to transfigure the facts of human experience and reality. In the past fifteen years or so, biblical studies has followed Parker's lead and adopted insights and methods derived from literary studies[2] and philosophical hermeneutics; but it has, to a great extent, refused to relinquish its rhetorical stance of value-free objectivism and scientific methodism.

This third literary-hermeneutical paradigm seems presently in the process of decentering into a fourth paradigm that inaugurates a rhetorical-ethical turn. This fourth paradigm relies on the analytical and practical tradition of rhetoric in order to insist on the public-political responsibility of biblical scholarship. It seeks to utilize both theories of rhetoric and the rhetoric of theories in order to display how biblical texts and their contemporary interpretations involve authorial aims and strategies, as well as audience perceptions and constructions, as political and religious discursive practices. This fourth paradigm seeks to engender a self-understanding of biblical scholarship as communicative praxis. It rejects the misunderstanding of rhetoric as stylistic ornament, technical skills or linguistic manipulation, and maintains not only "that rhetoric is epistemic but also that epistemology and ontology are themselves rhetorical."[3] Biblical interpretations, like all scholarly inquiry, is a communicative practice that involves interests, values, and visions.

Since the sociohistorical location of rhetoric is the public of the *polis*, the rhetorical paradigm shift situates biblical scholarship in such a way that its public character and political responsibility become an integral part of our literary readings and historical reconstructions of the biblical world. "The turn to rhetoric" that has engendered critical theory in literary, historical, political and social studies fashions a theoretical context for such a paradigm shift in biblical studies.[4] Critical theory, reader response criticism, and poststructuralist analysis,[5] as well as the insight into the rhetorical character and linguisticality of all historiography, represent the contemporary revival of ancient rhetoric.

The ethics of reading which respects the rights of the text and assumes that the text being interpreted "may say something different from what one wants or expects it to say"[6] is highly developed in biblical studies. Therefore, I will focus here on the ethics of biblical scholarship as an institutionalized academic practice. I will approach the topic by marking my present rhetorical situation as a "connected critic"[7] who speaks from a marginal location and that of an engaged position. Then I will explore the rhetoric of location and that of an engaged position. Then I will explore the rhetoric of SBL presidential addresses with respect to the shift from a scientific antiquarian to a critical-political ethos of biblical scholarship. Finally, I will indicate what kind of communicative practice such a shift implies.

Social Location and Biblical Criticism

In distinction to formalist literary criticism, a critical theory of rhetoric insists that context is as important as text. What we see depends on where we stand. One's social location or rhetorical context is decisive of how one sees the world, constructs reality, or interprets biblical texts. My own rhetorical situation is marked by what Virginia Woolf, in her book *Three Guineas*, has characterized as the "outsider's view":

> It is a solemn sight always—a procession like a caravanserai crossing a desert. Great-grandfather, grandfathers, fathers, uncles—they all went that way wearing their gowns, wearing their wigs, some with ribbons across their breasts, others without. One was a bishop. Another a judge. One was an admiral. Another a general. One was a professor. Another a doctor.... But now for the past twenty years or so, it is no longer a sight merely, a photograph . . . at which we can look with merely an esthetic appreciation. For there, traipsing along at the tail end of the procession, we go ourselves. And that makes the difference.[8]

Almost from its beginning women scholars have joined the procession of American biblical scholars.[9] In 1889, not quite one hundred years ago, Anna Rhoads Ladd became the first female member of this Society. Ten years later in 1899, Mary Emma Woolley, since 1895 chair of the Department of Biblical History, Literature and Exegesis at Wellesley College, and from 1900 to 1937 President of Mount Holyoke College, is listed in attendance at the annual meeting. In 1913 Professor Louise Pettibone Smith, who also served later in 1950–1951 as secretary of the Society, was the first woman to publish an article in the Journal of Biblical Literature. Mary J. Hussy of Mount Holyoke College had held the post of treasurer already in 1924–1926. At the crest of the first wave of American feminism, women's membership in 1920 was around 10 percent. Afterwards it steadily declined until it achieved a low of 3.5 percent in 1970. Presently the Society does not have a data base sufficient to compute the percentage of its white women and minority members.

The second wave of the women's movement made itself felt at the annual meeting of 1971, when the Women's Caucus in Religious Studies was organized, whose first co-chairs were Professor Carol Christ of AAR and myself of SBL. A year later, at the International Congress of Learned Societies in Los Angeles, the Caucus called for representation of women on the various boards and committees of the Society, the anonymous submission and evaluation of manuscripts for JBL, and the establishment of a job registry through CSR. At the business meeting two women were elected to the council and one to the executive board. Fifteen years later, I am privileged to inaugurate what will, it is hoped, be a long line of women presidents, consisting not only of white women but also women of color,[10] who are woefully under represented in the discipline. The historic character of this moment is cast into relief when one considers that in Germany not a single woman has achieved the rank of ordinary professor in one of the established Roman Catholic theological faculties.

However, the mere admission of women into the ranks of

scholarship and the various endeavors of the Society does not necessarily assure that biblical scholarship is done in the interest and from the perspective of women or others marginal to the academic enterprise. Historian Dorothy Bass, to whom we owe most of our information about women's historical participation in the SBL, has pointed to a critical difference between the women of the last century who, as scholars, joined the Society and those women who sought for a scientific investigation of the Bible in the interest of women.[11] Feminist biblical scholarship has its roots not in the academy but in the social movements for the emancipation of slaves and of freeborn women. Against the assertion that God has sanctioned the system of slavery and intended the subordination of women,[12] the Grimké sisters, Sojourner Truth, Jarena Lee, and others distinguished between the oppressive anti-Christian traditions of men and the life-giving intentions of God. Many reformers of the nineteenth-century shared the conviction that women must learn the original languages of Greek and Hebrew in order to produce unbiased translations and interpretations faithful to the original divine intentions of the Bible. Nineteenth-century feminists were well aware that higher biblical criticism provided a scholarly grounding of their arguments. Women's rights leaders such as Frances Willard and Elizabeth Cady Stanton were the most explicit in calling on women to learn the methods of higher biblical criticism in order to critique patriarchal religion.

Although Elizabeth Cady Stanton and the editorial committee of the *Woman's Bible* sought to utilize the insights and methods of "higher criticism" for interpreting the biblical texts on women, no alliance between feminist biblical interpretation and historical-critical scholarship was forged in the nineteenth century. Cady Stanton had invited distinguished women scholars "versed in biblical criticism" to contribute to the *Woman's Bible* project. But her invitation was declined because—as she states—"they were afraid that their reputation and scholarly attainments might be compromised."[13] This situation continued well into the first half of the century. In the 1920s Rev. Lee

Anna Starr and Dr. Katherine Bushnell, both outside the profession, used their knowledge of biblical languages and higher criticism to analyze the status of women in the Bible and the theological bases for women's role in scripture.[14]

The androcentric character of biblical texts and interpretations was not addressed by a woman scholar until 1964 when Margaret Brackenbury Crook, a longstanding member of the SBL and professor of Biblical Literature at Smith College, published *Women and Religion*.[15] Although Brackenbury Crook repeatedly claimed that she did not advocate feminism or animosity toward men but that as a scholar she was simply stating the facts on the basis of evidence, she did so in order to insist that the masculine monopoly in biblical religions must be broken and that women must participate in shaping religious thought, symbols, and traditions.

In the context of the women's movements in the seventies and eighties, women scholars have not only joined the procession of educated men but have also sought to do so in the interest of women. We no longer deny our feminist engagement for the sake of scholarly acceptance. Rather we celebrate tonight the numerous feminist publications, papers, and monographs of SBL members that have not only enhanced our knowledge about women in the biblical worlds but have also sought to change our methods of reading and reconstruction, as well as our hermeneutical perspectives and scholarly assumptions. The Women in the Biblical World Section has since 1981 consistently raised issues of method and hermeneutics that are of utmost importance for the wider Society.

And yet, whether and how much our work has made serious inroads in biblical scholarship remain to be seen. The following anecdote can highlight what I mean. I am told that after I had been elected president of the Society a journalist asked one of the leading officers of the organization whether I had been nominated because the Society wanted to acknowledge not only my active participation in its ongoing work but also my theoretical contributions both to the reconstruction of Christian origins and to the exploration of a critical biblical hermeneutic and rhetoric.[16] He reacted with surprise at such a suggestion and assured her that I was elected because my work on the book of Revelation proved me to be a solid and serious scholar.

Interpretive communities such as SBL are not just scholarly investigative communities, but also authoritative communities. They possess the power to ostracize or to embrace, to foster or to restrict membership, to recognize and to define what "true scholarship" entails. The question today is no longer whether women should join the procession of educated men, but under what conditions we can do so. What kind of ethos, ethics, and politics of the community of biblical scholars would allow us to move our work done in "the interest of women" from the margins to the center of biblical studies?

I hasten to say that I do not want to be misunderstood as advocating a return to a precritical reading and facile application of biblical texts on and about *Woman*. Rather I am interested in decentering it in a critical interpretive praxis for liberation. Ethos is the shared intellectual space of freely accepted obligations and traditions as well as the praxial space of discourse and action.[17] Since ethos shapes our scholarly behavior and attitudes, it needs to be explored more explicitly in terms of its practitioners. The rhetoric of previous addresses of SBL presidents can serve as a text for engaging us in a critical reflection on the ethos as well as the rhetorical aims of biblical studies.

The Rhetoric of Biblical Scholarship

Only a few presidential addresses have reflected on their own political contexts and rhetorical strategies. If my research assistant is correct,[18] in the past forty years, no president of SBL has used the opportunity of the presidential address for asking the membership to consider the political context of their scholarship and to reflect on its public accountability. Since 1947 no presidential address has explicitly reflected on world politics, global crises, human sufferings, or movements for change. Neither the civil rights movement nor the various liberation struggles of the so-called Third World, neither the assassination of Martin Luther King nor the Holocaust has become the rhetorical context for biblical studies. Biblical studies appears to have progressed in a political vacuum, and scholars seem to have understood themselves as accountable solely—as Robert Funk puts it—to the vested interests of the "fraternity of scientifically trained scholars with the soul of a church."[19] This ethos of American biblical scholarship after 1947 is anticipated in the following letter of R. Bultmann written in 1926:

> Of course the impact of the war has led many people to revise their concepts of human existence; but I must confess that that has not been so in my case. . . . So I do not believe that the war has influenced my theology. My view is that if anyone is looking for the genesis of our theology he [*sic*] will find, that internal discussion with the theology of our teachers plays an incomparably greater role than the impact of the war or reading Dostoievsky [*sic*].[20]

My point here is not an indictment of Bultmann, who more than many others was aware that presupposition-less exegesis is not possible nor desirable. Rather, it allows me to raise the question: Does the immanent discourse between teachers and students, between academic fathers and sons—or daughters, for that matter—between different schools of interpretation jeopardize the intellectual rigor of the discipline? Do we ask and teach our students to ask in a disciplined way how our scholarship is conditioned by its social location and how it serves political functions?

In his 1945 address, President Enslin of Crozer Theological Seminary ironizes the British snobbishness of Sir Oliver Lodge, who thought that the only American worth speaking to was Henry Cabot Lodge.[21] He nevertheless unwittingly supports such a scholarly in-house discourse by advocating an immersion in the works of the great scholars of the past while at the same time excoriating the "demand for the practical in biblical research." He rejects the requirement that biblical research "strengthen faith and provide blueprints for modern conduct" as one and the same virus which has poisoned German scholarship and made it liable to Nazi ideology. He therefore argues that biblical critics must be emotionally detached, intellectually dispassionate, and rationally value-neutral. Critical detachment is an achievement that turns the critic into a lonely hero who has to pay a price in comfort and solidarity. However, Enslin does not consider that this scholarly ethos of dispassionate industry, eternal questioning, utter loneliness, detached inquiry, patient toil without practical results, and the unhampered pursuit of truth "under the direction of men [sic] whom students can trust and revere" could be the more dangerous part of the same political forgetfulness that in his view has poisoned German biblical scholarship.

This scientist ethos of value-free detached inquiry insists that the biblical critic needs to stand outside the common circumstances of collective life and stresses the alien character of biblical materials. What makes biblical interpretations possible is radical detachment, emotional, intellectual, and political distanciation. Disinterested and dispassionate scholarship enables biblical critics to enter the minds and world of historical people, to step out of their own time and to study history on its own terms, unencumbered by contemporary questions, values, and interests. Apolitical detachment, objective literalism, and scientific value-neutrality are the rhetorical postures that seem to be dominant in the positivistic paradigm of biblical scholarship. The decentering of this rhetoric of disinterestedness and presupposition-free exegesis seeks to recover the political context of biblical scholarship and its public responsibility.

The "scientist" ethos of biblical studies was shaped by the struggle of biblical scholarship to free itself from dogmatic and ecclesiastical controls. It corresponded to the professionalization of academic life and the rise of the university. Just as history as an academic discipline sought in the last quarter of the nineteenth century to prove itself as an objective science in analogy to the natural sciences, so also did biblical studies. Scientific history sought to establish facts objectively free from philosophical considerations. It was determined to hold strictly to facts and evidence, not to sermonize or moralize but to tell the simple historic truth—in short, to narrate things as they actually happened.[22] Historical science was a technique that applied critical methods to the evaluation of sources, which in turn are understood as data and evidence. The mandate to avoid theoretical considerations and normative concepts in the immediate encounter with the text is to assure that the resulting historical accounts would be free of ideology.

In this country, Ranke was identified as the father of "the true historical method," which eschewed all theoretical reflection. Ranke became for many American scholars the prototype of the nontheoretical and the politically neutral historian, although Ranke himself sought to combine theoretically his historical method with his conservative political views.[23] This positivist nineteenth-century understanding of historiography as a science was the theoretical context for the development of biblical scholarship in the academy. Since the ethos of objective scientism and theoretical value-neutrality was articulated in the political context of several heresy trials at the turn of the twentieth century, its rhetoric continues to reject all overt theological and religious institutional engagement as unscientific, while at the same time claiming a name and space marked by the traditional biblical canon. Such a scientist posture of historical research is, however, not displaced when it is decentered by an objectivist stance that arrogates the methodological formalism of literary or sociological science. The pretension of biblical studies to "scientific" modes of inquiry that deny their hermeneutical and theoretical character and mask their historical-social location prohibits a critical reflection on their rhetorical theological practices in their sociopolitical contexts.

Although the dominant ethos of biblical studies in this century seems to have been that which is paradigmatically expressed in Bultmann's letter and Enslin's address, there have nevertheless also been presidential voices that have challenged this self-understanding of biblical scholarship. Already in 1919, James Montgomery of the University of Pennsylvania had launched a scathing attack on the professed detachment of biblical scholars when addressing the Society:

We academics flatter ourselves on what we call our pure science and think we are the heirs of an eternal possession abstracted from the vicissitudes of time. We recall Archimedes working out his mathematical problems under the dagger of the assassin, or Goethe studying Chinese during the battle of Jena. But we dare not in this day take comfort in those academic anecdotes nor desire to liken ourselves to the monastic scholars who pursued their studies and meditations in their cells undisturbed by the wars raging without. . . .[24]

Almost twenty years later, at the eve of World War II, Henry Cadbury of Harvard University discussed in his presidential address the motives for the changes in biblical scholarship. He observed that most members of the Society are horrified by the perversions of learning and prostitutions of scholarship to partisan propagandistic ends in Nazi Germany. He noted, however, that at the same time most members are not equally aware of the public responsibility of their own scholarship and of the social consequences of their research. He therefore challenged the membership to become aware of the moral and spiritual needs in contemporary life and to take responsibility for the social and spiritual functions of biblical scholarship.[25]

At the end of World War II, Leroy Waterman of the University of Michigan also called in his address for the sociopublic responsibility of scholarship. Biblical scholarship must be understood as situated in a morally unstable world tottering on the brink of atomic annihilation. Students of the Bible should therefore take note of the deep moral confusion in their world situation and at the same time make available "any pertinent resources within their own keeping." While biblical scholars cannot forsake their research in "order to peddle their wares," they also cannot remain in the ivory tower "of privileged aloofness."

Waterman argued that biblical studies and natural science have in common the "claim to seek truth in complete objectivity without regard to consequences."[26] But biblical scholarship and natural science sharply diverge with respect to their public influence. Whereas science has cultivated a public that is aware

117

of the improvements science can effect for the increase of human welfare or its destruction, biblical scholarship has taken for granted the public influence of the Bible in Western culture. Therefore, it has cultivated as its public not a society as a whole but organized religion, "whose dominant leadership has been more concerned with the defense of the status quo than with any human betterment accruing from new religious insights."[27] The task of biblical studies in this situation is therefore to make available to humanity on the brink of atomic annihilation the moral resources and ethical directives of biblical religions. At the eve of the Reagan-Gorbachev summit on nuclear arms reduction, Waterman's summons of the Society to public responsibility is still timely.

The Ethos of Biblical Scholarship: Critical Rhetoric and Ethics

Although I agree with his summons to public responsibility, I do not share his optimistic view of positive science. The reluctance of the discipline to reflect on its sociopolitical location cannot simply be attributed, as Waterman does, to the repression of biblical scholarship by organized religion. It is as much due to its ethos of scientist positivism and professed value-neutrality. Scientist epistemologies covertly advocate an apolitical reality without assuming responsibility for their political assumptions and interests. "Scientism has pretensions to a mode of inquiry that tries to deny its own hermeneutic character and mask its own historicity so that it might claim a historical certainty."[28]

Critical theory of rhetoric or discursive practices, as developed in literary, political, and historical studies, seeks to decenter the objectivist and depoliticized ethos of biblical studies with an ethos of rhetorical inquiry that could engage in the formation of a critical historical and religious consciousness. The reconceptualization of biblical studies in rhetorical rather than scientist terms would provide a research framework not only for integrating historical, archaeological, sociological, literary, and theological approaches as perspectival readings of texts but also for raising ethical-political and religious-theological questions as constitutive of the interpretive process. A rhetorical hermeneutic does not assume that the text is a window to historical reality, nor does it operate with a correspondence theory of truth. It does not understand historical sources as data and evidence but sees them as perspectival discourse constructing their worlds and symbolic universes.[29]

Since alternative symbolic universes engender competing definitions of the world, they cannot be reduced to one meaning. Therefore, competing interpretations of texts are not simply either right or wrong,[30] but they constitute different ways of reading and constructing historical meaning. Not detached value-neutrality but an explicit articulation of one's rhetorical strategies, interested perspectives, ethical criteria, theoretical frameworks, religious presuppositions, and sociopolitical locations for critical public discussion are appropriate in such a rhetorical paradigm of biblical scholarship.

The rhetorical understanding of discourse as creating a world of pluriform meanings and a pluralism of symbolic universes, raises the question of power. How is meaning constructed? Whose interests are served? What kind of worlds are envisioned? What roles, duties, and values are advocated? Which social-political practices are legitimated? Or which communities of discourse sign responsible? Such and similar questions become central to the interpretive task. Once biblical scholarship begins to talk explicitly of social interests, whether of race, gender, culture, or class, and once it begins to recognize the need for a sophisticated and pluralistic reading of texts that questions the fixity of meaning, then a *double ethics* is called for.

An *ethics of historical reading* changes the task of interpretation from finding out "what the text meant" to the question of what kind of readings can do justice to the text in its historical contexts. Although such an ethics is aware of the pluralism of historical- and literary-critical methods as well as the pluralism of interpretations appropriate to the text, it nevertheless insists that the number of interpretations that can legitimately be given to a text are limited. Such a historical reading seeks to give the text its due by asserting its original meanings over and against later dogmatic usurpations. It makes the assimilation of the text to our own experience and interests more difficult and thereby keeps alive the "irritation" of the original texts and their historical symbolic worlds that they relativize not only them but also us. By illuminating the ethical-political dimensions of the biblical text in its historical contexts, such an *ethics of historical reading* allows us not only to relativize through contextualization the values and authority claims of the biblical text but also to assess and critically evaluate them.

The rhetorical character of biblical interpretations and historical reconstructions, moreover, requires an *ethics of accountability* that stands responsible not only for the choice of theoretical interpretive models but also for the ethical consequences of the biblical text and its meanings. If scriptural texts have served not only noble causes but also to legitimate war, to nurture anti-Judaism and misogynism, to justify the exploitation of slavery, and to promote colonial dehumanization, then biblical scholarship must take the responsibility not only to interpret biblical texts in their historical contexts but also to evaluate the construction of their historical worlds and symbolic universes in terms of a religious scale of values. If the Bible has become a classic of Western culture because of its normativity, then the responsibility of the biblical scholar cannot be restricted to giving "the readers of our time clear access to the original intentions" of the biblical writers.[31] It must also include the elucidation of the ethical consequences and political functions of biblical texts in their historical as well as in their contemporary sociopolitical contexts.

Just as literary critics have called for an interpretive evaluation of classic works of art in terms of justice, so students of the Bible must learn how to examine both the rhetorical aims of biblical texts and the rhetorical interests emerging in the history of interpretation or in contemporary scholarship. This requires that we revive a responsible ethical and political criticism which recognizes the ideological distortions of great works of religion. Such discourse does not just evaluate the ideas or propositions of a work but also seeks to determine whether its very language and composition promote stereotypical images and linguistic violence. What does the language of a biblical text "do" to a reader who submits to its world of vision?[32]

In order to answer this question, the careful reading of biblical texts and the appropriate reconstruction of their historical worlds and of their symbolic universes need to be complemented by a theological discussion of the contemporary religious functions of biblical texts which claim scriptural authority today in biblical communities of faith. To open up biblical texts and the historical reconstructions of their worlds for public discussion requires that students learn to traverse not only the boundaries of theological disciplines but also those of other intellectual disciplines.[33]

To enable students to do so, biblical studies will have to overcome the institutionalized dichotomy between graduate training in the university and ministerial education in schools of theology. M.A. and Ph.D. students interested in teaching in seminaries and church-related schools are to become skilled in critical-theological reflection just as M.Div. and D.Min. students should be versed in the analysis of religion and culture. Moreover, in view of the insistence that all professions and research institutions should become conscious of the values they embody and the interests they serve, students in religious studies as well as in theology must learn to engage in a disciplined reflection on the societal and public values[34] promoted by their intellectual disciplines.

Finally, the growth of right-wing political fundamentalism and of biblicist literalism in society, religious institutions, and the broader culture feeds antidemocratic authoritarianism and fosters personal prejudice. In the light of this political situation, biblical scholarship has the responsibility to make its research available to a wider public. Since literalist biblical fundamentalism asserts the public claims and values of biblical texts, biblical scholarship can no longer restrict its public to institutionalized religions and to the in-house discourse of the academy. Rather, biblical scholarship must acknowledge the continuing political influence of the Bible in Western culture and society.

If biblical studies continues to limit its educational communicative practices to students preparing for the professional pastoral ministry and for academic posts in theological schools, it forgoes the opportunity to foster a critical biblical culture and a pluralistic historical consciousness. Therefore, the Society should provide leadership as to how to make our research available to all those who are engaged in the communication of biblical knowledge, who have to confront biblical fundamentalism in their professions, and especially to those who have internalized their oppression through a literalist reading of the Bible. Such a different public location of biblical discourse requires that the Society actively scrutinize its communicative practices and initiate research programs and discussion forums that could address issues of biblical education and communication.

In conclusion: I have argued for a paradigm shift in the ethos and rhetorical practices of biblical scholarship. If religious studies becomes public deliberative discourse and rhetorical construction oriented toward the present and the future, then biblical studies becomes a critical reflection on the rhetorical practices encoded in the literatures of the biblical world and their social or ecclesial functions today. Such a critical-rhetorical paradigm requires that biblical studies continue its descriptive-analytic work utilizing all the critical methods available for illuminating our understanding of ancient texts and their historical location. At the same time, it engages biblical scholarship in a hermeneutic-evaluative discursive practice exploring the power/knowledge relations inscribed in contemporary biblical discourse and in the biblical texts themselves.

Such an approach opens up the rhetorical practices of biblical scholarship to the critical inquiry of all the disciplines of religious studies and theology. Questions raised by feminist scholars in religion, liberation theologians, theologians of the so-called Third World, and by others traditionally absent from the exegetical enterprise would not remain peripheral or nonexistent for biblical scholarship. Rather, their insights and challenges could become central to the scholarly discourse of the discipline.

In short, if the Society were to engage in a disciplined reflection on the public dimensions and ethical implications of our scholarly work, it would constitute a responsible scholarly citizenship that could be a significant participant in the global discourse seeking justice and well-being for all. The implications of such a repositioning of the task and aim of biblical scholarship would be far-reaching and invigorating.

Appendix 3

Evaluation, Commitment, and Objectivity in Biblical Theology

James Barr

[Note: This text is reproduced from *The Concept of Biblical Theology: An Old Testament Perspective* (London: SCM, and Minneapolis: Fortress, 1999), 189–208, with the permission of the author and of SCM Press and Fortress Press. It has been edited slightly and the notes have been adapted for inclusion in the present volume.]

One important element of biblical theology has been the conflict between those who think of it as an "objective" discipline which describes what historically was the theology of biblical people, and those who think of it as a faith-committed discipline. This latter view insists on personal religious involvement. In addition, it tends to assert that biblical theology should not only state what was there in biblical times but should provide interpretations for the present day. Interpretations for the present day require, however, personal identification with the life and needs of the present-day community of faith.

We may begin by noting that this particular question is one of the most hotly disputed in all biblical theology, and especially so in the modern American discussion. The "cool, descriptive" historical and objective position was classically stated by Krister Stendahl in a famous article in *The Interpreter's Dictionary of the Bible*.[1] Central representatives of the contrary view have been, at an earlier stage, James Smart, and, more recently, Brevard Childs.[2] Very strong opinions, often approaching personal insults, have been expressed. Smart not only said that Stendahl was wrong about this but went on to suggest that his teaching had gone far towards destroying his students' ability to interpret the Bible. "Why," he asked, "do the preachers of today, trained by the Stendahls in biblical exegesis, find a veritable abyss between the Then and the Now, between the original meaning and the contemporary meaning, an abyss which they did not even discover until they were faced with the task of preaching?"[3] Childs for his part asserts outright that Stendahl's approach "destroys from the outset the possibility of genuine theological exegesis"[4]—a drastic judgment on one of the greatest exegetical thinkers of twentieth-century America.[5] Given this atmosphere, it will not be easy to achieve sweet reasonableness or compromise.

There seem to be the following different elements involved in the argument for faith-commitment:

(1) Biblical theology deals with revelation, and so its data and contours are not perceptible except to (or through) committed faith. An "objective" approach makes this sort of insight unattainable.

(2) Biblical theology should not simply "describe objectively" what was there in the Bible but should evaluate it, explain why it is good and show how it is a positive theological resource.

(3) Biblical theology should not only state what was there in biblical times but should provide an interpretation for modern times or at least the key to, or the method for, such an interpretation.

(4) The biblical theologian is the servant of the modern community of faith and cannot fulfil this task except through sharing in the faith of that community.

In favor of the faith-commitment approach one must say that it is the one that fits in better with modern ideas, at least in much of the world of religion. In it the person who claims to speak "with objectivity" is likely to be laughed at: objectivity is an old idea, a outmoded fallacy long ago exploded.[6] Everyone, it is thought, has some kind of personal "agenda" that he or she is pursuing. Not only is this so, but this is how it ought to be. It is fashionable to emphasize existential involvement and political activism and to look with scepticism at all thoughts of "objectivity." The argument for faith-commitment thus has the wide support of current popular ideology.

This opinion may surprise some and may indeed be disputed. Nevertheless I think it is right. I was surprised therefore to find that Ollenburger thinks that Stendahl's opinions have been generally accepted:

> They have profoundly affected the way biblical theologians, particularly in this country, think about their work and reflect on certain central, methodological questions. In fact, the distinctions for which Stendahl pleaded have come to be seen as virtually axiomatic, and self-evidently so, particularly for distinguishing biblical from systematic theology and the other theological disciplines. It is in locating biblical theology within the theological curriculum, and in providing a rationale for this location, that Stendahl's proposal has proved most persuasive.[7]

This may be right, but my impression is the opposite. I have heard far more dissent from Stendahl's position than acceptance of it; and, as he himself saw it, his proposal was deliberately made as in *opposition* to what was normal among biblical theologians. I certainly do not agree that his ideas have been seen as "virtually axiomatic": this seems to me remote from reality. I am more inclined to agree with Walter Brueggemann's opinion that Stendahl's distinction between "what it meant" and "what it means" is "increasingly disregarded, overlooked, or denied"[8]—whether such a judgment is right or wrong.

It is certainly possible that the "curricular location of biblical theology," as referred to by Ollenburger, has had a certain resemblance to Stendahl's ideas. Biblical theology is indeed commonly taught for the most part—rightly in my opinion—as a study of the theology implied in the context of biblical times and cultures. This, however, is not necessarily the result of persuasion by Stendahl's arguments. It could be the effect rather of classroom practicalities. For faith-commitment cannot easily be introduced as an essential into the classroom situation unless all participants are of the same faith, and indeed the same form of the same faith, in which case biblical theology would have to become an explicitly denominational activity. It is not easy to insist on faith-commitments as an essential in biblical theology when one is instructing a class that includes some Lutherans, some Anglicans of different currents, some Barthians, some progressive/liberationist/feminist Presbyterians, some Roman Catholics, some conservative Baptists, some liberal Methodists, some Mennonites and Disciples of Christ, perhaps two or three Jews and a few enquirers who are searching for a faith rather than possessing one. If pedagogical practice has seemed to agree with Stendahl's ideas, this may be a result of such educational practicalities rather than the influence of his arguments. Indeed these same practicalities may well have been an important factor in the formation of Stendahl's own mind, for he has been an experienced educational administrator as well as a theologian.

Even where scholars have found that educational practice made it easier or necessary to teach along something like part of Stendahl's lines, I think that many of these scholars remained personally unwilling to adopt his principles as their own. In spite, therefore, of respect for Ollenburger's opinion, I continue to think that the common ideology is more on the side of faith-commitment.

Moreover, it can be argued that faith-commitment has the support of present and recent practice on its side in another way. In general, one must say, the whole operation of biblical theology, like that of biblical exegesis as a whole (including critical and historical exegesis), has been massively driven and motivated by faith. There have been exceptions here and there, but as a whole the enterprise has been the work of persons who understood themselves to be standing behind the Bible, identifying with its essentials, and advancing its potentialities for the nourishment of faith and true religion. And—to start at the lowest level of argument—how many people, if they were without lively religious faith and uninterested in the life of synagogue or church, would be likely to want to become involved in biblical theology at all? Biblical theology is likely to continue as a field of faith and commitment through sheer lack of interest from any other quarter. The vision, sometimes conjured up, of numerous sceptics and agnostics entering biblical theology and seeking to write Theologies of the Old or New Testament, is not a serious cause for worry.[9] People interested in biblical theology are likely to continue to be religious believers, as they always have been.

This, however, does not prove that faith-commitments are logically or methodologically necessary for the operations which biblical theology in fact undertakes. We may begin by illustrating this from the case of Th. C. Vriezen's *Outline of Old Testament Theology*.[10] In his extensive introductory section he emphasizes the essential place of faith and the task of evaluating the Old Testament by theological standards and seeking the element of revelation in it. But when we turn to the content section, which occupies the main part of his volume, it is not clear what parts of that discussion actually depend upon faith or commitment. So far as I can see, though occasional final evaluations and comments may be so dependent, the general exposé of material and the main argument do not so depend at all. In principle, anyone could do it. The following statements are typical of Vriezen's work:

> The holiness of God does not only imply a consciousness of his unapproachableness, his being completely different, his glory and majesty, but also his *self-assertion*. (302)

> This idea of the jealousy of Yahweh is closely connected with the religious exclusiveness of the religion of Israel and must be recognized as inherent in Yahwism; it is the main cause of the development of theoretical monotheism, which does not only forbid the worship of other gods but also denies their existence. (303)

Such observations, whether right or not, seem not to have any logical dependence on the faith of the writer or reader: they are comments that any intelligent and interested person who had read the Old Testament might make.

Later, in the "canonical approach" of Childs, something of the same kind happens. As we have seen, he strongly rejects the "cool, descriptive, historical" approach supported by Stendahl (which will be discussed in more detail below). According to Childs, it "destroys from the outset the possibility of genuine theological exegesis."[11] The arguments which he puts forward at this point are three. First, that "the text must be seen as a witness beyond itself to the divine purpose of God"; secondly, that "the analogy between the two [Testaments] is to be sought on the ontological [as over against a historical] level"; and thirdly, that "there must be movement from the level of the witness to the reality itself." These arguments may be quite reasonable in themselves, though I shall later question their relevance to this point in the dispute. Stendahl answers reasonably and moderately,[12] saying that these points made by Childs are "useful formulations of the step from the descriptive to the normative and theological," but do nothing to substantiate Childs' main point, i.e. "the fallacy in isolating the descriptive task." Childs' own canonical approach is said to belong within faith-committed Christian theology. This would suggest that it contained insights that would be invisible or untenable for anyone without this commitment.

But what happens in fact is otherwise. The actual procedures of the canonical approach are methods that can be adopted by anyone, whether they have theological commitment or not. In effect, many of them were accepted by literary critics who thought it right to move in this direction, but who were by no means believers in the theological sense. Believing in the virtues of a literary canon, being interested in the final form of the text and not in its historical location, and seeking a holistic "construal" of the whole, they could follow out or produce exactly the same kinds of exegesis. It must have been an embarrassment to Childs to find his proposals supported from this quarter.[13] Like Vriezen before him, Childs was not able, or did not try, to point to interpretative decisions made under his method which could not have been made by intelligent unbelievers interested in canonical and holistic method. Moreover,

Childs' argument, if valid, must count not only against Stendahl's view but against that of Eichrodt and, indeed, against those of many leading representatives of biblical theology.

Incidentally, the reader should bear in mind that Childs may have either changed his mind about some of this, or contradicted himself. In his later work *Old Testament Theology in a Canonical Context*, 12, he tells us that

> the canonical approach envisions the discipline of Old Testament theology as combining both descriptive and constructive features. It recognizes the descriptive task of correctly interpreting an ancient text which bears testimony to historic Israel's faith. Yet it also understands that the theological enterprise involves a construal by the modern interpreter, whose stance to the text affects its meaning.[14]

But this (with some question perhaps about the final phrase) is just what Stendahl maintained. Exactly both these steps were the center of his proposal. The only difference might be over how much of one or the other is to be included under the term "biblical theology." Certainly they are so close here that, if Stendahl's proposal destroys the possibility of theological exegesis, the same is true of Childs' own, and Childs owes him an apology for the very drastic judgment he expressed. In view of many other passages, it might seem more likely that the opinion expressed in *Old Testament Theology* as quoted above was a slip and that Childs' original statement represents his continuing position. But in his still later *Biblical Theology of the Old and New Testaments*, Childs discusses the need "to *describe* carefully both the continuity and discontinuity between these two different witnesses of the Christian Bible."[15] He points out the variety of modes in which Old Testament and New Testament materials may be related to one another. Then he continues: *"Only after this descriptive task has been done* will it be possible to turn to the larger task of trying to engage in theological reflection of [sic!—is "on" meant?] the whole Christian Bible in the light of its subject matter of which it is a witness" (my italics). He goes on to refer to the following sections of his massive work "as part of this descriptive task." How does this differ from Stendahl's program?

In this respect the position of Eichrodt seems to be more accurate in defining what has actually happened in biblical theology. The subject, according to him, is not dependent on faith or on any special mode of cognition, but lies within the field of traditional Old Testament studies: it differs from historical studies not through moving to a different plane altogether but only in that it is structural or systematic rather than diachronic (and, of course, as I have argued, structural study of this sort was always inherent in historical study in any case, so that there is at the most only a difference of emphasis). The operation works in the same way and on the same logical basis as any other of the normal scholarly operations practiced by Old Testament scholars. In other words, though Eichrodt himself did not express it in exactly this way, it no more depends on faith-commitment than does historical criticism or any other operation of biblical scholarship.[16]

To put it in another way: it may be argued that theology by its nature depends on faith and revelation. Of course. But this applies only to theology proper, "authentic" or "real theology"; it is for the moment uncertain, however, whether biblical theology can necessarily claim to be theology in the authentic sense at all, and therefore the argument cannot yet be legitimately extended to it.

Put it again in these terms: it can be said that biblical theology is part of Christian theology, and several have argued in this way. But the argument is indecisive. For there is both a wider and a narrower definition of what is comprised in "Christian theology." In a narrower sense it may be that "Christian theology" means "Christian doctrinal theology" or "Christian practical theology," and in that case one might argue that one cannot work in that area without personal faith and commitment (though even then it would be a stiflingly narrow and exclusivist view, which many active theologians would repudiate). But in the wider sense "Christian theology" would include all the subjects studied in a course of Christian theological study. These would include such disciplines as church history or Hebrew grammar, and it is doubtful whether personal faith and commitment is a necessity for serious work in these areas. Biblical theology might be like church history, or it might be like history of doctrine. Thus just to claim that it is "part of Christian theology," even if true, does not prove anything. Christian theology in the wider sense includes many subjects which can be studied, and indeed must be studied, independently of personal faith. In order to justify the claim that one cannot work in biblical theology without personal faith-commitments, it has to be shown that there are observations, insights and conclusions that could not be made by persons who did not have these commitments. Thus far this has not been shown, or indeed been attempted. The material thus far written under the heading of biblical theology—including the material written by those who insist on a faith-commitment—suggests the reverse: that it requires an *interest* in theology and an *empathy* with it, but not a personal faith-commitment.

What might with more justice be said in favor of faith-commitment is something else: namely, that a biblical theology worked out with a faith-commitment will be a somewhat different biblical theology from that written with the cool, objective, descriptive approach. The argument is not for or against a biblical theology but for or against a particular *kind* of biblical theology. Thus, to cite again Childs' sentence written against Stendahl, "that the text must be seen as a witness beyond itself to the divine purpose of God" simply does not touch the intended target: for Stendahl's proposal stands whether Childs' objection is true or not. The point raised by Stendahl's position is: even if the text is seen as a witness beyond itself, how do we know what it is witnessing to? We have to know what the theology of the text is before we can tell what aspect of "the divine purpose of God" it is saying something about. Childs' objection therefore stands only if it is already known what "the divine purpose of God" is. It is therefore an argument not for theological exegesis as such, but for his own personal theological position, or, more precisely, a call for all biblical theologians to

133

presuppose that by their own personal faith they know exactly what the divine purpose of God is.

There is another way in which the difference between accurate "description" and faith-related "commitment" to the "normative" tends to dissolve in practice. Obviously, for those who hold a strong enough view of the authority of the Bible, if something is a good "description" of biblical beliefs and attitudes, then it is *ipso facto* "normative" and they are committed to it. In terms of method of discovery, there is no difference. Sermons, for instance, which by their own nature are appeals for commitment, contain constant claims that they are giving an accurate description of persons, entities, situations and doctrines of the Bible. Those who assume "committed" faith-attitudes are continually uttering what they claim to be accurate descriptions of situations within the Bible. Because they are accurate descriptions, they are normative. The difference is not one of method in the knowledge of the biblical situation, but one of the view of biblical authority. This is why those who deplore the idea of description continually return to using it themselves.

The same applies in another aspect, namely the special position of *Old Testament* theology. For how can a theology of *part* of the Old Testament, or even of the whole of it, be "normative" *in itself* for Christianity? How can it be normative for Christianity except as it is considered in relation to the New Testament and the basic patristic sources of Christian theology? It would obviously be reasonable to think of it as normative for the Jewish reader, but for the Christian it could hardly be normative in itself, unless one takes the view that all theological positions of the Old Testament are *identical* with those of the New and with those of mature Christian theology. Unless this is so, one would have to have a view of the "normative" which is itself relative: that is, it is normative *in so far as* any Old Testament information, taken in itself, can be normative for Christianity. Here again the question of normativity is not an indication of a *method* or attitude with which to approach the theology, but is rather a function of the view of biblical authority with which one works. And even within the most orthodox currents of theological tradition such views are numerous and variable.

Another way in which our problems can be formulated is by use of the *temporal* distinction of past and present, the distinction between "what it meant" and "what it means." This distinction is best known from the famous and clear—or perhaps one should say "at first sight fairly clear"—formulation of it by Krister Stendahl. Stendahl thought that biblical theology in itself should not be primarily evaluative. According to his view,[17] biblical theology is a descriptive undertaking which, historically, and as objectively as possible, tells us what sort of "theology" existed in ancient times. "Objectively" here means: independently of whether one advocates this theology or disapproves of it, or thinks it is the ultimate divine revelation, or thinks it does not matter. These issues do not matter: we are concerned only with knowing what was there at the appropriate stage in biblical times. What the corresponding biblical texts mean for our time is a different affair.

Take, let us say, the New Testament picture of a world of demons: it would be very wrong if we allowed our description of that time to be affected by the question whether or not we ourselves think it is good to believe in demons or a personal devil for today. We have to say, as honestly as we can, what *they* thought at the time.

Or, to take the example which actually, I believe, was very seminal in forming Stendahl's mind on this matter: the role of women in the church. When the ordination of women was discussed, a commission of the Church of Sweden discussed the matter and came to the conclusion that, on the basis of the New Testament, there was no case for women's ordination.[18] Stendahl agreed that, as descriptive biblical theology of the New Testament regarding this matter, this was quite correct. But, he thought, this was not decisive for the present day. A multitude of factors had altered the social setting since New Testament times: simply to repeat the New Testament judgment in modern times would be to falsify it. Thus it would be wrong, just because one thought the ordination of women to be right for the present day, to read back this opinion into the New Testament and to obscure the theology of the matter which they had actually held. It would be equally wrong, just because one knew (correctly) that the New Testament opinion was against this sort of thing, to suppose that this in itself settled the interpretative issue for modern times. Biblical theology is in principle historical and descriptive; the move to interpretation for the present day is a separate matter and involves other factors. Biblical theology concerns "what it meant"; a further and different hermeneutical step is involved in deciding "what it means." Such is the position taken by Stendahl.

Stendahl's own work illustrates the problems very well. His study on the place of women in the church has been a major example; to this we may add two others of his most important areas of impact on biblical interpretation: first, his support for an emphasis on bodily resurrection and his opposition to the idea of immortality of the soul, and secondly his essay on "The Apostle Paul and the Introspective Conscience of the West."

In the matter of resurrection and immortality,[19] Stendahl maintains that the biblical books show little, or practically no, interest in the immortality of the soul, and says that this result is the product of "cool, descriptive biblical theology"—exactly the correct terms of his own program as described above. But in fact his thoughts on the matter are very deeply and passionately intermingled with what, as he sees it, "it means." He thinks—or then thought, for he might have adjusted his opinion later—that people nowadays have factually lost interest in the immortality of the soul, that they *were right to lose interest in* it, and that it is *good for them* that they have done so or will do so. I believe I have shown that these strongly held sentiments about the modern relevance of the theme have distorted his treatment of the biblical material itself.[20]

In the second case Stendahl basically argues that St. Paul in his thoughts about "justification by faith" was talking about something very different from the introspective problems of individual sin and guilt which became the dominant Western inheritance from Paul especially after Augustine and Luther.[21] A shift to an understanding of what Paul was "really" talking about—the status of communities in relation to the church—would clearly, in Stendahl's mind, be very salutary for modern theology and religion. Here, without claiming to be an expert, I think that Stendahl is very likely right, and I do not see that his convictions about the present have distorted the biblical evidence. On the other hand, it cannot be doubted that, on this occasion, "what it means" is very much mixed up with "what it meant," and it is the importance of the modern message perceived that has in part prompted and fired this particular presentation of "what it meant."

Stendahl's principle is thus somewhat compromised in its actual working out. Nevertheless in general he is emphatically in the right in this whole matter, although certain modifications will be suggested below. It would be quite wrong to suppose that, even if he had not universally succeeded in maintaining the distinction for which he pleads, this shows that the distinction is wrong. On the contrary, the fact that we are able to criticize his exegesis on these grounds shows that his principle is right. It would be fatal to biblical theology if every worker in the field felt at liberty to "discover" in the biblical material whatever message or implication he or she thought to be "good for" modern humanity to hear. Individual failures on Stendahl's part to observe his own principle do not at all prove that the principle is wrong: indeed, the possibility of detecting that they are failures is dependent on the rightness of the principle itself.

Particularly important is the principle in those cases where there is some element in the Bible which is distasteful to the biblical theologian. "I don't much like this, why shouldn't I leave it out?" is a temptation that many of us have felt from time to time. That it can be successfully resisted is shown by Stendahl's own work on the place of women in the church. He was himself convinced that women should be ordained, that this was theologically right. But he made it clear that he agreed with the view of the Swedish theological commission, to the effect that the biblical evidence, taken for itself, pointed in the opposite direction.

This recognition of a difference between what one oneself believes and what one perceives to have been the case in the Bible can be illustrated from other instances. Thus Albert Schweitzer is often credited with having discredited the "liberal" picture of the historical Jesus, and justifiably so. But it would be wrong to suppose that Schweitzer's own theology was opposed to liberalism. On the contrary, he was very much a liberal. But he was able to paint the picture of the "eschatological fanatic" Jesus, one quite dissimilar to his own belief. We can conjoin with him the name of Johannes Weiss. Heikki Räisänen rightly takes them as an example of how relative (not absolute) objectivity works: "they dared to paint a Jesus who held a faith different from their own."[22]

To put it in another way, a hermeneutic that will tell us "what it means" for today must be prepared to include an element of *critique*. This aspect has been missed by many biblical theologians, because they thought that, the more deeply the biblical theology was probed, the more obviously, directly and profoundly it will supply the correct and relevant meaning for today. Again Stendahl grasped this point well. Characteristic biblical theology of the 1940s and 1950s, he thought, worked out the biblical or Hebraic thought-forms of biblical times, indicated the complicated network of concepts and ideas that they implied, and then dumped the whole thing on the lap of twentieth-century theology, declaring that it was all authoritative as it stood and had to be accepted as such. And, in spite of the alleged "decline" of biblical theology, some people are still doing the same. As I have just said, Stendahl himself to some extent did it with the immortal soul.

This view of Stendahl's, indeed, has been much resisted by others. The opposition has argued, perhaps, from two angles, different but perhaps complementary. On the one hand, the ideal of objective description has been contested: the Bible could not be studied with cold objectivity, one could not enter into it without personal involvement and decision. According to this point of view, objective historical examination is illusory. James Smart went so far as to suggest that the ideal of objectivity is an actual *obstacle* to the discovery of truth about the Bible, and that passionate commitment was the sure way to true knowledge a notion that flies in the face of all experience of the workings of religious enthusiasm.

On the other hand, biblical theology, it has been argued, is above all a mode in which the Bible is made more alive and relevant for today. Much of the discussion of the subject has shown the influence of homiletic needs and the pressure of rhetorical techniques: if one can come to perceive certain aspects as central to the Bible, how can one possibly rest content with observing that fact and not at once go out to proclaim that essential message to modern humanity? And, if biblical theology cannot show us how to preach the Christian message for today, what use is it?[23] Note the emphasis on *utility* implied by this part of the argument.

Actually, of course, it may well be that biblical theology will have a great deal of utility for questions of today. Nevertheless the approach to it must not be governed by expectations of utility, otherwise these considerations will inevitably corrupt its accuracy in representing the biblical material itself.

In any case, even continuing with the matter of utility, arguments depending on faith-commitment are bound to lose their own utility if they are honestly presented as such. For those, whether scholars or preachers or laypersons, who build an argument on the basis of biblical material and add, "of course, this is the biblical view *only because* I approach it as a faith-committed liberal or evangelical, or Lutheran or Presbyterian," have in effect destroyed their own argument and its utility. For the faith-commitment arguments to have force and utility, they have to be presented *as if* they were built upon the descriptive model which the faith-commitment supporter denies.

Stendahl's argument has sometimes been so read as if to suggest that, in his opinion, biblical scholarship should do nothing to provide interpretation for today.[24] It should have been obvious that this was not so. His whole scheme was intended precisely to provide interpretation for today, and clearly did so in all the three cases I have cited above. Arguments against his thinking on the ground that it is "purely historical" or "antiquarian" or the like are complete misrepresentations. The center of his scheme is that there are two distinct stages: we have to know correctly what the theology of the Bible was before we go on to state its meaning for the present day. This first stage he calls "biblical theology," but the naming of it does not seem to be so essential. It would not much alter Stendahl's scheme if we were to use "biblical theology" for the two stages combined, so long as the distinction between them were clearly observed. But in using "biblical theology" strictly for the first stage only Stendahl was, I suggest, following the main line of what has been understood by this term in the twentieth century. In interpreting for the present day we have to be clear and honest in indicating those points at which the modern interpretation is distinct from the theology of ancient times.

Stendahl's position has often been misunderstood, and a discussion of some of these misunderstandings may be helpful. It seems to be misunderstood by Matitiahu Tsevat, a Jewish scholar whose important contributions to our subject deserve to be better known. He takes the investigation of "what it meant" to be, for Stendahl, purely history of religion, while "what it means" is real and normative Christian theology.[25] The reverse is the case: for him the biblical theology was the objective description of the theology as it existed in biblical times. The move to "what it means" for today is the task of a hermeneutic procedure which can lead to results that are, at least on the surface, very different from "what it meant" in biblical times. The hermeneutic procedure very definitely takes into account the changed situation of people in medieval and modern times.

Another possible misunderstanding of Stendahl occurs in Friedrich Mildenberger's article "Biblische Theologie versus Dogmatik?"[26] He works mainly from Stendahl's early paper in Hyatt, *The Bible in Modern Scholarship*. He appears to think that

Stendahl is attacking the possibility of dogmatic thinking and insisting that his own historical descriptive method is final. Actually Stendahl is seeking to *limit* the claims of biblical theology, which he describes as (at least potentially) "imperialistic," in order to increase the freedom of dogmatics to take decisions which lie beyond the proper scope of biblical theology. This is an important positive emphasis, in view of the tendency of biblical theology to raise itself from the position of an ancillary discipline to one of superior authority over all other forms of theology.

A grosser and more serious misrepresentation of Stendahl's thought appears in Francis Watson's *Text, Church and World.*[27] He follows an early reaction of Childs in describing Stendahl's position as "a naive empiricism" (33). Stendahl's argument "is important not because it is original but as a clear statement of the self-understanding of most practitioners of historical-critical exegesis" (31). Watson emphasizes the contrast between the descriptive task, which is relatively simply and straightforward ("we can all join in and check each other's results against the original," 30), and the task of interpretation for the present day, "an arduous road towards a goal that we glimpse only from afar." The emphasis is on "the autonomy of the historical task and on the need for great circumspection in undertaking the theological one" (31).

All of this is wrong. First of all, "naive empiricism" is mere abuse, for I do not see anything empirical in Stendahl's approach. It presupposes, if anything, the categories of biblical theology and of hermeneutics as then understood, and if it has a fault it lies on that side aud not in "empiricism." Nowhere, so far as I can see, does Stendahl speak of, or advocate, an empirical procedure. Nor does Stendahl state the self-understanding of practitioners of historical-critical exegesis. Historical criticism, as a matter of fact, scarcely enters into his presentation. His position is predicated upon the concept of biblical theology. Admittedly, he does not make it very clear how one reaches that biblical theology in the first place. But his main point is that if there is a biblical theology, then it is a theology that existed in the past. This would be the same for a biblical theology built upon a quite anti-critical basis, denying historical criticism entirely: it would still, as purporting to be a biblical theology, be a theology intended as the theology of the people of biblical times.

Again, if Stendahl's position was "a clear statement of the self-understanding of most practitioners of historical-critical exegesis," it is surprising that most such practitioners found it highly controversial and were unable to agree on whether they supported it or not.

Moreover Watson's criticism on the grounds that for Stendahl theological assessment and construction were extremely remote and difficult of access is obviously untrue. As has been shown by all the examples I have put forward, the matter of ordination of women, the matter of soul and immortality, and the matter of justification by faith, Stendahl was swift to perceive and express present-day theological decisions arising from biblical exegesis. On one of these matters, that of justification by faith, the importance of his initiative for contemporary theology has been widely recognized by a variety of exegetes, including Watson himself, as indicated above.

Historical critics, Watson alleges, "find that theology subjects the text to alien norms" (32). The reality, however, is quite the reverse: it is the tradition of biblical theology itself, as we have seen, that has repeatedly emphasized the danger that (traditional) theology subjects the text to alien norms.

Watson asserts that historical-critical description "is dependent on a prior interpretation of these texts as historical artefacts—chance remnants of a previous stage of human history whose meaning is wholly determined by their historical circumstances of origin" (33). Of course they are historical artefacts—even Watson probably does not deny this—but his argument is really that they are understood as *only* historical artefacts and nothing more at all, having *no meaning* at all beyond their historical circumstances of origin. This is rubbish and only shows how far the force of his argument has made him remote from the actualities of the people he is talking about.

Finally, Watson instructs us:

> To appeal for an autonomous "description" is to ignore the fact that there is no such thing as a pure description of a neutral object; description always presupposes a prior construction of the object in terms of a given interpretative paradigm (33).

How amazingly original a thought! Who in the hermeneutical discussion has not heard it proclaimed a hundred times? To suppose that Stendahl, who had his finger uniquely on the pulse of exegetical discussions, was unaware of this elementary argument is only one part of the contemptuous superiority with which Watson approaches his subject.

In spite of my support for Stendahl's position, however, there are important modifications and corrections which ought to be suggested. In particular, I shall argue that his definition of biblical theology was excessively hermeneutical in character. It was dependent on a hermeneutical model based on *meanings*—"what it meant" against "what it means"—and on a hermeneutical model that is faulty.

On the one hand it is somewhat misleading to define the object of biblical theology as "what it meant." Probably Stendahl did not intend his distinction to be taken too exactly: for him the point was the distinction between "meant" and "means," and the temporal distinction is very clearly conveyed by his formula. But the word "meant" suggests the meaning of the text, or of the Bible; in ancient times, what it then meant to people. What it meant to people could be a variety of things, but in any case it does not seem to coincide with the *theology* of the Bible (or of its various texts). Biblical theology is not looking for what it *meant*, but for *what it was*: what the theology of the Bible, or underlying the Bible, was (or perhaps *is?*—for it could be argued that, if a biblical theology can be discovered and stated, then that theology not only *was* but is and *remains* the theology of the Bible). The question is therefore about the "it" rather than about the tense of "means" or "meant." If Stendahl's formula had been expressed in this way, it might have received wider acceptance.

A more serious and far-reaching observation is this: what "it" means (for the present) is never in fact what the Bible alone means. Theological interpretation of the Bible for today, which is what Stendahl had in mind, is never interpretation of one thing only, namely the Bible. In this assertion there are two elements. First, interpretation for today is interpretation in which the Bible is related to other relevant elements: the theological traditions, philosophy, modern religious and social situations and—very likely—natural theology. Or, to put it more vividly, it is not we who interpret the Bible but the Bible which interprets us and our world: cf. the title of Perlitt's article "Auslegung der Bibel—Auslegung der Welt." What is normally intended when we talk about interpretation for today is not interpretation of the Bible alone.

This means—still more important—that the model of an interpretation which takes the ancient biblical message or material and transfers or translates this into the modern world is a mistaken one—not only from the historical but also from the religious/theological point of view. This is not a new idea, for it has been explored by Dietrich Ritschl and others, but its potential is as yet insufficiently realized.

We cannot take an ancient passage or an ancient work like the Bible and say that its meaning has to be updated, brought into the modern world. "What it meant" in Stendahl's terms is its *only* meaning. The process of religious appropriation of the Bible is not that we produce a new meaning, "what it means" for today. It is, on the contrary, that we, the modern religious community, sink ourselves increasingly into its *past* meaning. In the doing of this, that past meaning, which is the only meaning, interprets and criticizes our modern life as it comes into contact with our modern thoughts, traditions, experiences and histories. This process can inaccurately be called the finding of "the meaning of the Bible for today" but it is not really that, for the Bible has this "new" meaning only because it is brought into contact with a mass of non-biblical knowledge (or pseudo-knowledge). In other words, we are saying that the traditional idea of hermeneutics, as applied in much modern theology, has worked in a biblicistic manner, as if the thing being interpreted was (uniquely) the Bible and the process involved was (uniquely or primarily) one of overcoming the temporal distance and producing from the one source, the Bible, a meaning *of that source* for today.

These thoughts, if valid, are of great importance for our general subject. For they mean that the religious appropriation of the Bible is much closer, much more analogous, to the historical study of it than has generally been perceived. It is not at all that the religious use of the Bible is identical with the research of the historian or the historical critic, but the historian's penetration into biblical times is a more technical and methodically controlled process which operates in a mode analogical to the basic religious use of "what it meant." In this respect Stendahl was mistaken in expressing his distinction, in itself a right one, in terms related to the "actualizing" hermeneutics then current. And, to forestall an obvious objection, the analogy with *theology* is also valid. The tendency to place *theology* in serious contrast with *history*—a tendency very visible in much biblical theology and particularly so in Childs' canonical approach—is certainly a deep contradiction. This is shown not so much by abstract arguments about history and theology but above all by the fact that the very approach which so sets theology apart from history is one whose theology is overwhelmingly *historical* in character. Childs' own argumentation, as is obvious, is not really theological argumentation, but is above all historical argumentation, which uses the history of theology as a grid upon which value judgments are fixed.[28]

There remains one other criticism of Stendahl's formulation which is also relevant for other wide areas of biblical theology. The question is: can the term "descriptive" be accepted for use without further qualification? Let us agree with the term "descriptive" as against the opposing faith-commitment position. And let us accept that the description of the (implied) theology of the Bible is the aim of biblical theology. Stendahl is therefore basically in the right. But his term "descriptive" does not well describe the process by which the work has to be done. The reality with which biblical theology is concerned is not an accessible entity, the contours of which are readily available for description. The process is essentially an *imaginative* one, which involves imaginative *construction*. It is indeed historical, as Stendahl rightly puts it, in the sense that it works within a historical framework and is subject to historical questioning and verification; but historical description, without the additional specification of imaginative construction, will not suffice to provide an answer. If Stendahl had modified his formula in this sense, some of the objections voiced against it might have been avoided.

Again, it may be questioned whether "description" is the right term for some of the relations that biblical theology seeks to express. Given an entity with an apparent unity, one may speak of "describing" aspects of that entity: thus, let us say, we may try to describe the tendencies of the book of Deuteronomy or the thought of the prophet Amos, or to describe how terms for "soul" and "spirit" are used throughout the Bible, if there is in fact some unity in this group of terms. But the relations between the Old and New Testaments are not an entity of that kind. To use "describe" as the term for the way in which one may seek to relate the Old Testament to the New is a strange use of language. Thus it is not surprising that Preuss in the concluding sentences of his recent Old Testament Theology looks back on his main work as one of "pure description" but goes on to add: "the discovery and unfolding of these basic structures of Old Testament faith can . . . not remain only a historically orientated and purely descriptive [undertaking]." For then he goes on to speak of a "biblical theology" (in my terms a pan-biblical theology) which would open out into the basic structures or structural analogies of the complete (Christian) Bible. The perception and expression of these larger structures and wider analogies seems to go beyond what can be properly counted as "description."

Moreover, description requires the use of terms and categories belonging to *our modern* speech. Only in the most extreme formalistic approaches can we describe biblical texts and realities without some reference to our own categories. Formalism can be valuable because it gives us some important data, but for most purposes we have to go beyond that. If we set out to "describe" the meaning of Hebrew *nephesh,* we can do much of value with sheer statistics, with syntactical matrices, with parallelisms and so on, but we soon come to a point where we use English words of today, and then we have to start explaining that it does not mean exactly "soul" (and there is a question what that word means in English today, if it means anything) and yet in certain contexts it really *is* rather like "soul" after all—a familiar exercise to everyone who tries to talk about such things. There is an unavoidable element of *comparison* with the way we think about things today, whether religiously or unreligiously.[29] And so "description" of ancient things involves a certain critical examination of modern things, and "what it meant" comes to be somewhat mixed up with what something or other means today.

We have to discuss more fully the matter of objectivity.[30] Those who insist on faith-commitment are commonly very hostile to the idea of objectivity, and argue that perfect objectivity is an unrealistic notion which cannot be realized in this world. Everyone who says anything has some purpose or agenda which influences and possibly distorts the subject spoken about. Quite so. But this argument is irrelevant, for we are not speaking about perfect objectivity. We are speaking about the willingness to seek *some limited but adequate measure* of objectivity. We are asking for the admission that some limited degree of objectivity is better than a complete abandonment of objectivity. The faith-commitment argument is commonly so extremely hostile to objectivity that it is unwilling to set any limits at all to prejudice, special pleading and propaganda. Thus fairness and open-mindedness are seldom mentioned in works on biblical theology. Stendahl's argument does not ask for perfect objectivity or for the objectivity of natural science. But it does ask, and rightly, that the person of faith-commitment should, in the face of the biblical material, to some extent hold his or her faith-commitment in suspense, place it, as it were, in a state of questioning, in which one asks oneself: does the biblical material really fit in with my existing faith-commitment, or may it be that my faith-commitment has to be adjusted in view of my new insights into the biblical material?

There is another way in which the anti-objectivist arguments should be discounted. They are, as we have seen, part of the set of existentialist ideas which have been so influential in the entire base of biblical theology (and in many quarters are now being superseded by "postmodern" ideas, which are slightly different). It should not be believed, however, that these ideas are employed consistently. A consistent anti-objectivism might well be found in Bultmann; but just at this point many Old Testament theologians will turn away from him and look in another direction. Barthianism, which, as we have seen, was more influential in Old Testament theology, has also often had an anti-objectivist air and has opposed the supposed objectivist aims of historians. But Barthians who follow this line are not against objectivity all the way. They deny it to historians for a quite different reason: it is not that they are against objectivity—on the contrary, they are in favor of it—but that they want it for themselves. That the Barthian theological vision has objectivity has been a basic conviction, and the same is true of the canonical approach as developed by Childs. Unquestionably much of the attraction of the canonical approach lies in the impression that here, in the canon, at last, in contrast with the varieties and speculative theories of critical interpretation, we have something *objective* as a foundation. The tirades of biblical theologians against objectivity are therefore by no means always to be taken too seriously.

That these have inner contradictions can easily be seen. In his *Introduction to the Old Testament as Scripture*, Childs announces that it "seeks to describe as objectively as possible the canonical literature." But his Exodus commentary began with a solemn declaration that he "does not share the hermeneutical position of those who suggest that biblical exegesis is an objective, descriptive enterprise."[31] In his later *Biblical Theology of the Old and New Testaments* he tells us that he attempts in this volume "to focus in more detail on the descriptive task of relating the Old Testament witness to the history of Israel, of course, according to its canonical form" (101). He wants to "describe" a trajectory of psalmic tradition (92). He refers to "a careful descriptive reading of the two Testaments in reference to the law" (551). However, he refers disparagingly to a "purely descriptive, sociological explanation" as the "least satisfactory approach" to questions about the historical Jesus (604). Referring to Hermisson's study of faith, he tells us that "the appeal within the Old Testament to a reality called faith is a feature constitutive of Christian theology and is hardly a neutral descriptive reading of the literature" (617). These contradictions are a surface symptom of a contradiction about objectivity in deep structure. Those who despise and attack the value of objectivity are desperately in need of it for themselves.

Another matter that may be mentioned in this connection is the question of the "time-conditioned quality" of interpretation. It has often been argued that attempts at "objective" work involved the illusion of standing outside the stream of time and producing a result wholly independent of one's own modern position. This argument is often used in order to discredit historical-critical studies. It is one of the many myths thought up by the fertile imaginations of anti-historical writers. For, of course, it is entirely untrue that the great historical critics like Harnack, or the great theorists of critical history like Troeltsch, had any such idea of themselves. And as applied in justification of more modern exegetical proposals, the notion is a hypocritical one. Thus to take one example, Childs uses this argument repeatedly (e.g., "the canonical approach . . . rejects a method which is unaware of its own time-conditioned quality").[32] But nowhere in the literature of the canonical approach are we told that this novel approach is conditioned by the background of the writer and by the social, economic and political situations of the period 1960–1990. Still less are we told that the value of the canonical approach will be merely one phase which will last for one generation at most, and that by the end of that time people will all have become historicists again or return to some other non-canonical stance. In fact the "time-conditioned" argument is an important element in the present-day trend towards complete relativism, which rightly distresses Childs. But if it distresses him, he should not use the arguments that sustain it. Arguments like this were used because they seemed to be a good stick with which to beat the historical emphasis; those who used them often did not consider how they would rebound upon themselves.

A conclusion to this difficult controversy may now be attempted. First, as I have said, few are likely to embark on biblical theology without a faith-commitment. If any do, well, that is fine. They may surely be welcomed, for they may well come upon insights which the religious believer might not think of. Biblical theology should certainly not seek to be a religiously or denominationally closed and exclusive preserve. But, if most workers certainly work from a faith position, their faith-commitment in this case can properly be only a commitment to discover what is really there in the Bible, even if what is found disagrees with our present faith-commitments, extends them in a quite unexpected way, or goes in a quite different direction from them. Otherwise commitment tends very easily to mean that we see in the Bible what we already consider to be right, or useful, or in agreement with a particular church tradition, or relevant, or "good for" other people or useful for preaching. Examples of this are richly demonstrable in the literature of biblical theology. In this sense Stendahl's position, though in part wrongly expressed, seems to be right. It is particularly important in the sort of cases on which he himself worked, cases where the biblical evidence reveals something that seriously clashes with current faith-commitments. On the other hand, those who have opposed Stendahl have often spoken as if faith-commitments meant that everything in the Bible must be directly right, acceptable, relevant and authoritative just as it stood. The value of his ideas appears best when we consider cases where this is not so.

A good example is the case of natural theology. For many twentieth-century Christians—if they are theologically trained, since otherwise they will probably never have heard of the question—it is a faith-commitment that natural theology is totally wrong. But what if there are passages in the Bible which use natural theology and depend upon it? Those who oppose Stendahl's position will also tend to ignore these passages, or to explain them away, or to deny their obvious meaning. This may then be an indirect denial of an important element of scripture. Now it may still be a right faith-commitment to say that natural theology is wrong. But if so, Stendahl's approach provides a way of working. One can state and describe historically a body of ideas that are there in the Bible, while at a separate (doctrinal or hermeneutic) stage one will have to explain how or why these elements are of limited value, or limited to their own time, or in some other way not finally authoritative. (I myself would not do this, but this is just an explanation of a possible example.)

Thus it is far from the case that the task of biblical theology is to explain what the text "means for the present day" or how it fits with the various more recent theological traditions or how it determines what should be done about modern socio-ethical questions. It is far from the duty of the biblical scholar to judge on these matters, though of course he or she may incidentally do so. This is, or should be, the judgment of the church or religious community itself. The church has plenty of people who are competent and ready to tell whether an interpretation of a part of the Bible is meaningful for the present day, or whether it fits in with Lutheran, Calvinist, Methodist or Catholic traditions, or what it means for modern social questions. All these people are ready and willing to be heard. What the church requires from biblical scholars is not that they should join them in this vociferous pleading, but that they should make clear how far these various resultant interpretations, whether apparently "relevant" or not, whether in accord with church tradition or not, whether socially meaningful for today or not, are firmly based in the Bible itself. Biblical scholars, therefore, whatever their allegiance in these matters, work usefully in so far as they ask the question: granted that I believe this or that to be in accord with my theological tradition, to be relevant for today, to be socially and ethically desirable, my duty to the church or community is to put into brackets, into parenthesis, these my own convictions and to ask whether or not the Bible itself supports them. If it does, then one can continue as one has been; if not, then a process of theological change may have to begin.

The apparent conflict between personal commitment and objective description is therefore a poor model,[33] which can lead only to severe and irreconcilable conflicts between opposed and partially valid positions. In essence, faith-commitment requires and supports a search for adequately objective description.

Notes

Notes to Chapter 1

1. A. Race, *Christians and Religious Pluralism: Patterns in the Christian Theology of Religions* (Maryknoll, NY: Orbis, 1983), 1.

2. F. F. Segovia, "'And They Began to Speak in Other Tongues': Competing Modes of Discourse in Contemporary Biblical Criticism," in *Reading from this Place, Vol. 1: Social Location and Biblical Interpretation in the United States* (ed. F. F. Segovia & M. A. Tolbert; (Minneapolis: Fortress, 1995), 1–32, 1. Segovia speaks of "the increasing diversity and globalization of the discipline, as more and more new voices, more and more perspectives and standpoints, entered the field." "The world of biblical criticism today is very different from that of the mid-1970s."

3. Elisabeth Schüssler Fiorenza, "The Ethics of Biblical Interpretation: Decentering Biblical Scholarship," *JBL* 107 (1988): 3–17 [reprinted as Appendix 2 in this volume].

4. Ibid., 9.

5. R. S. Sugirtharajah, "Inter-faith Hermeneutics: An Example and Some Implications," in *Voices from the Margin: Interpreting the Bible in the Third World* (ed. R. S. Sugirtharajah; new ed.; London: SPCK, 1995), 306–18, 306–7.

6. Ibid., 317.

7. L. Schottroff, "Working for Liberation: A Change of Perspective in New Testament Scholarship," in *Reading from this Place, Vol. 2: Social Location and Biblical Interpretation in Global Perspective* (ed. F. F. Segovia & M. A. Tolbert; Minneapolis: Fortress, 1995), 183–98, 194, 188.

8. Segovia, "And They Began," 1, speaks of the "swift demise of the historical-critical model."

9. The following catena of quotations stems from writings which I, on the whole, greatly esteem. I just think that on this par-

ticular (but central) point these generally perceptive critics are barking up the wrong tree.

10. Schüssler Fiorenza, "Ethics," 5.

11. R. S. Sugirtharajah, "Introduction," *Voices from the Margin: Interpreting the Bible in the Third World* (ed. R. S. Sugirtharajah; (London: SPCK, 1991), 1.

12. Schüssler Fiorenza, "Ethics," 10–11,13; cf. G. M. Soares-Prabhu, "Laughing at Idols: The Dark Side of Biblical Monotheism (An Indian Reading of Isaiah 44:9–20)," *Reading from this Place, Vol. 2,* 109.

13. Schüssler Fiorenza, "Ethics," 11; cf. M. A. Tolbert, "When Resistance Becomes Repression: Mark 13:9–27 and the Poetics of Location," *Reading from this Place, Vol. 2,* 331–46, 341.

14. F. F. Segovia, "Cultural Studies and Contemporary Biblical Criticism: Ideological Criticism as Mode of Discourse," *Reading from this Place, Vol. 2,* 1–17, 17.

15. Sugirtharajah, "Afterword," in *Voices from the Margin* (new ed. 1995), 457–73, 460.

16. Kwok Pui Lan, "Response to the *Semeia* Volume on Post-colonial Criticism," *Semeia* 75 (1996): 211–17, 212–13. This accusation leaves many a critic as baffled as his customary biblicist critics who routinely accuse him of precisely the opposite heresy. The same is true of the claim that historical critics treat "the canon and the texts as fixed, stable, and privileged points of 'origin'," whereas post-colonial critics now "examine the cultural and historical processes that call them into being" (ibid., 213). I had always thought that I was, along with many others, examining various historical and cultural processes! I should add that I profoundly agree with Kwok Pui Lan's main concerns (biblical interpretation as "dialogical imagination" and "liberating the Bible") in her article "Discovering the Bible in the Non-biblical World," in *Voices from the Margin* (new ed. 1995), 289–305.

17. Kwok Pui Lan, "Response," 212–13.

18. Segovia, "Cultural Studies," 6.

19. Segovia, "And They Began," 8.

20. Ibid., 13. Segovia (ibid., 12) does realize that the "historical-critical model" contains quite different movements, but he nevertheless lumps them all together.

21. Ibid., 29.

22. Ibid., 13.

23. R. S. Sugirtharajah, "Postscript," *Voices from the Margin* (1991), 434–44, 436.

24. Krister Stendahl, *Meanings: The Bible as Document and as Guide* (Philadelphia: Fortress, 1984), 11–44; the article on 'Biblical Theology' was originally published in 1960 [reprinted as Appendix 1 in this volume]. Ironically, Stendahl's slogan is expressly rejected by the Krister Stendahl Professor at Harvard: Elisabeth Schüssler Fiorenza, *Revelation: Vision of a Just World* (Edinburgh: T & T Clark, 1993), 1.

25. For James Barr, *The Concept of Biblical Theology: An Old Testament Perspective* (London: SCM, 1999), 300, "the existence of biblical theology . . . proves that historical criticism has not had a monopoly." On the attacks of the former against the latter; cf. ibid., 15 and passim. W. Eichrodt already spoke of the "tyranny of historicism in OT study" (see ibid., 25–6.). Yet scholars such as Eichrodt certainly belong to the "historical critics" as perceived by present-day liberationists. The "biblical theology" movement was part of the historical paradigm; it is this branch that mainly embodies many of the dangers perceived by liberationist interpreters (such as the condemnation of other religions).

26. Barr, *Concept*, 205, correctly speaks of "a consistent anti-objectivism" on their part. [See Barr's essay "Evaluation, Commitment, and Objectivity in Biblical Theology," reprinted from his *The Concept of Biblical Theology* as Appendix 3 in this volume.]

27. This is clear in the case of M. S. Enslin, "The Future of Biblical Studies," *JBL* 65 (1946): 1–12, esp. 6–9, castigated for "scientist ethos" by Schüssler Fiorenza, "Ethics," 10. It is somewhat surprising to find Enslin and Henry Cadbury (Schüssler Fiorenza, ibid., 12) placed into opposite camps in the debate, considering Cadbury's classic caveat for the "peril of modernizing Jesus" in the heyday of the Social Gospel movement. How does this differ from Enslin's warning of the longstanding "peril of the demand for the practical in biblical research" ("Future," 6)? Enslin rightly complained that "what is demanded today is that we provide a warm religious approach," while stressing that he himself was "all in favor of genuine religion" (ibid., 8). In another connection he confessed his "love" for the Bible: see *Christian Beginnings* I (New York: Harper, 1956; orig. ed. 1938), ix. Cf. Krister Stendahl, *The Final*

Account (Minneapolis: Fortress, 1995), 21: "A greedy hunger for relevance often blinds the eyes of preachers and theologians." See also note 58 below.

28. Barr, *Concept*, 196.

29. Today one might add: or the political position implied.

30. Ibid., 205.

31. Ibid., 206 (Barr here criticizes "biblical theologians" such as Brevard Childs). In his effort to disclose the allegedly imperialist ('colonial') nature of classical exegetical scholarship, Sugirtharajah grossly overinterprets individual statements by some scholars. Thus he quotes the opening lines of Georg Strecker, *Die Bergpredigt* (Göttingen: Vandenhoeck & Ruprecht, 1984; English translation: *The Sermon on the Mount: An Exegetical Commentary* (Nashville: Abingdon, 1988), 9: "No proper exegesis of the Sermon on the Mount can ignore the results of more than two hundred years of historical critical research into the New Testament." He takes this to mean that Strecker

> rules out at the outset the right [!] of a reader or an interpreter to use any other means to understand the text, and those who do not practice these methods are seen as outside the circle. The implication is here that the Western academy sets the ground rules for interpretation and defines what tools shall be used, and these are paraded as universally applicable in opening up the text. Anyone who does not employ them or does not engage with them is seen as an outcaste. The inference is that any culturally informed reading by a Gandhi, a Tilak, a Krishnapillai is ruled out. (Afterword, 460).

This assessment does not do justice to Strecker; cf. in particular his "Ausblick" (181–90, esp. 187–90.) He there speaks of the vital political importance of the discussions about the Sermon on the Mount. The contribution of a New Testament scholar "kann hierzu keine endgültigen und umfassenden Entscheidungshilfen beisteuern" (no "universal" claims here!):

> Sein Beitrag zur Diskussion kann jedoch dazu verhelfen, durch exegetische Analyse die Textgrundlage besser zu verstehen und hierdurch kritische Kriterien bereitzustellen. . . . Übereinstimmung mit dem ursprünglichen

Wortsinn ist ein nur begrenzt gültiges Wahrheitskriterium. Im Einzelfall kann gerade die Abweichung vom wörtlich Gebotenen den Gehorsam im Geist bedeuten, wie man es etwa an Dietrich Bonhoeffers einsamer Entscheidung zum Widerstand im dritten Reich verwirklicht sieht. (Ibid., 187–88).

Strecker even mentions Gandhi (briefly, to be sure) in his account of history of interpretation—not as an "outcaste," but rather in a positive tone along with Tolstoy, Martin Luther King and Helmut Gollwitzer. Tolstoy (who inspired Gandhi), definitely not a historical scholar, is, despite some criticisms, given credit for taking up Matthew's concern (concrete commands are to be fulfilled): ibid., 15–16, 189.

32. Barr, *Concept*, 80. See also Barr, "Modern Biblical Criticism," in *The Oxford Companion to the Bible* (ed. B. M. Metzger & M. D. Coogan; Oxford University Press, 1993), 318–24.

33. Barr, "Criticism," 320, points out that "historical investigation is only one of the aspects of traditional criticism." What he finds most important is "the general intellectual atmosphere of criticism, with its base in language and literary form, its reference grid in history, and its lifeblood in freedom to follow what the text actually says. . . ." (ibid., 324)

34. Cf. Barr, *Concept*, 662–63 n. 22: "Stendahl's position is that there are two distinct *operations*, not that the second stage should or must be left to some other group of persons. " (Barr's italics.) Schüssler Fiorenza (*Revelation,* 1) takes the "prevailing division of labor" to mean that "scientific exegesis has the task of elaborating what the text . . . *meant* whereas practical theology and proclamation must articulate what it *means* today." Stendahl himself points out that his essays "often move from the descriptive task to the development of meaning for church and society today" (*Meanings,* 7). In view of the criticism by Segovia ("Cultural Studies," 13) that (in his view, unlike historical criticism) "cultural studies calls for critical analysis of all readers and readings, whether located in the academy or not, highly informed or not," it should be noted that Stendahl wrote a perceptive and appreciative article on the Book of Mormon (*Meanings,* 99–113).

35. Stendahl, *Meanings,* 1 (my italics).

36. Ibid., 2.

37. Barr, *Concept*, 204. See pp. 202–208, where Barr modifies Stendahl's statement in a useful way.

38. Schüssler Fiorenza, *Revelation*, 117. In what follows I draw on my Manson memorial lecture, "Liberating Exegesis?" *BJRL* 78 (1996): 193–204, 194–98.

39. Schüssler Fiorenza, *Revelation*, 122.

40. Ibid., 126.

41. Ibid., 122.

42. Ibid., 79–80.

43. Ibid., 68.

44. Ibid., 95.

45. Ibid., 119–20.

46. Rev 13:8, 12, 14 (all dwellers on earth will worship the Beast); 13:8, 17:8 (their names are not found in the book of life). John thirsts for vengeance on all "dwellers on earth" (6:10), for slaves no less than for kings (6:15); cf. also 8:13, 11:10, 17:2. All non-Christians seem demonized. John expects that eventually those who keep their faith intact will receive "power over the Gentiles" and "rule them with an iron rod" (2:26).

47. Cf. Schüssler Fiorenza's exegesis of Rev 11:13, 15:3-4 and 21:17-21 in *Revelation*, 79, 91–92, 112.

48. Schüssler Fiorenza, "Ethics," 14.

49. Schüssler Fiorenza, *Revelation*, 123f. Interestingly, there is a palpable tension between Schüssler Fiorenza's liberationist and feminist concerns. She notes that 'Jezebel' of Thyatira is the first Christian woman who has fallen victim to "vilifying intra-Christian rhetoric" (ibid., 134), and yet her idealization of John's perspective prevents her from fully rehabilitating this remarkable woman leader, who seems to me to be a lot more open to 'cosmopolitanism' than John is. On 'Jezebel' and other Christians attacked by John, see my articles "The Nicolaitans," *ANRW* II.26.2 (1995), 1602–44, and "The Clash Between Christian Styles of Life in the Book of Revelation," *StudTheol* 49 (1995): 151–66.

50. L. Thompson, *Revelation: Apocalypse and Empire* (Oxford: Oxford University Press, 1990); idem, *Revelation* (Nashville: Abingdon, 1998). Cf. A. Y. Collins, "Persecution and Vengeance in the Book of Revelation," *Apocalypticism in the Mediterranean World and the Near East*, ed. D. Hellholm (2nd ed.; Tübingen: J. C. B. Mohr, 1989) 729–49, 746; J. Ulrichsen, *Das eschatologische Zeitschema der*

Offenbarung des Johannes (Oslo, 1988), 44–47; H.-J. Klauck, "Das Sendschreiben nach Pergamon und der Kaiserkult in der Johannesoffenbarung," *Bib.* 73 (1992): 153–56, 160–64.

51. Schüssler Fiorenza does not deny any of this. Her answer is that John's perception of the situation was not shared by everyone; his perception is that of the suffering majority (*Revelation*, 125–27). It was "only the provincial elite and the Italian immigrants" who were "reaping the wealth of the empire's prosperity" (ibid., 100). Most people "were suffering from the widening gap between rich and poor." If Revelation stresses the exploitation and oppression perpetrated by Rome's imperialist power, then it expresses an assessment that was not shared even by all Christians (ibid., 127). Actually, John belongs to "a cognitive minority within the Christian community of Asia" (ibid., 138). But this correct observation renders the overall picture drawn by Schüssler Fiorenza suspect—for are we to conclude that the majority of Asian Christians (such as the authors and addressees of the Pastorals, Luke-Acts or 1 Peter) belonged to the small privileged elite? The attempt to make John a cosmopolitan spokesman for the vast majority of people (who differs from the vast majority of Christians in his environment) does not carry conviction.

52. Ibid., 132.

53. This is what Tolbert, "Resistance," 343–44, does in her equally liberation-oriented discussion of Mark 13, even though the synoptic apocalypse would seem somewhat less extreme than Revelation in its vision. She admits that Mark 13 "calls for the utter destruction of the world and everyone in it who is not among the elect."

54. Cf. G. Theissen, "Antijudaismus im Neuen Testament—ein soziales Vorurteil in heiligen Schriften," *Für ein neues Miteinander von Juden und Christen* (ed. J. Thierfelder & W. Wölfing; Weinheim: Deutscher Studien Verlag, 1996), 77–97.

55. Interpretations which portray Paul as standing in a relatively strong continuity to Jewish faith, presented by J. D. G. Dunn and many others, are effectively refuted by K. Kuula, *The Law, the Covenant and God's Plan I: The Polemical Treatment of the Law in Galatians* (Helsinki: The Finnish Exegetical Society, 1999).

56. I have met more than one postgraduate reader of Moore's *Judaism 1–3* (1927–30) who has taken for granted that Moore (a

Presbyterian) was a Jew, because he speaks in such a favorable tone of Judaism.

57. E. P. Sanders, *Paul and Palestinian Judaism* (London: SCM, 1977).

58. It should be noted that M. S. Enslin, accused of a scientist ethos by Schüssler Fiorenza, was one of those Christian scholars who early on displayed a positive understanding of Judaism; see his *Christian Beginnings I* (1938), esp. vii, 99–100. Contrast the out-of-hand dismissal of basic Jewish values by Sugirtharajah (of all people!): "Inter-faith Hermeneutics," 312–13, criticized by H. Räisänen, *Marcion, Muhammad and the Mahatma* (London: SCM, 1997), 4–5.

59. N. Beck, *Mature Christianity: The Recognition and Repudiation of the Anti-Jewish Polemic of the New Testament* (Selingsgrove, 1985), 261.

60. J. Levenson, *Sinai and Zion: An Entry into the Jewish Bible* (Minneapolis: Fortress, 1985), 109 n. 37.

61. L. Donaldson, "Postcolonialism and Biblical Reading: An Introduction," *Semeia* 75 (1996): 1–14, 11; cf. J. Weaver, "From I-Hermeneutics to We-Hermeneutics: Native Americans and the Post-Colonial," ibid., 153–76, 159.

62. R. A. Warrior, " A Native American Perspective: Canaanites, Cowboys, and Indians," *Voices from the Margin* (1991), 277–85.

63. N. Ateek , "A Palestinian Perspective: Biblical Perspectives on the Land," *Voices from the Margin* (1991), 267–76.

64. Donaldson, "Postcolonialism," 12.

65. Ibid.

66. D. J. A. Clines, *Interested Parties: The Ideology of Writers and Readers of the Hebrew Bible* (JSOTSS 205; Sheffield: Sheffield Academic Press, 1995).

67. "Good indeed is the god of the law who envied the Canaanites to give to the Israelites their land, houses they had not built and olive trees and fig trees they had not planted." The citation is preserved by Epiphanius and quoted in A. von Harnack, *Marcion* (Darmstadt: Wissenschaftliche Buchgesellschaft; 1985; orig. ed. 1921), 281.

68. Ibid., 220. On Harnack's view of the Old Testament which is almost always misrepresented (it was *not* a question of outright "rejection") see my *Marcion*, 76–7.

69. G. Lüdemann, *The Unholy in Holy Scripture: The Dark Side of the Bible* (London: SCM, 1997), e.g. 54.

70. Soares-Prabhu, "Laughing at Idols."

71. Ibid., 113.

72. Ibid., 123–24.

73. Note also the harsh but justified judgment (ibid., 125):

> What makes the biblical authors so prone to see and condemn idolatry in others is the element of idolatry in their own religion. . . . An image does not have to be material. . . . Yahweh who cannot be represented by a material image is in fact thought of in a mental image, cast in the likeness of a human male . . . one who even leads his people to war, destroys their enemies, and demands strict "ethnic cleansing" to guard against their possible religious apostasy. . . ."

Without knowing Soares-Prabhu's article, I made a similar point in *Marcion*, 46–7 (with reference to W. C. Smith and his experience of India). Soares-Prabhu ("Laughing," 127–28) refutes the common perception of Second Isaiah as a prophet of universalism, the evidence for which he finds meager. Historical critics may attribute the satire in 44:9-20 to someone other than Second Isaiah himself, but even so the moral problem remains.

74. Ibid., 129–30.

75. Soares-Prabhu here misleadingly uses the word 'anti-Semitism'.

76. Ibid., 131 (my italics).

77. In any case, some scholars of Deuteronomy have done something along these lines by pointing out oppressive features (and some of their later effects) in Deuteronomy, especially B. Lang, "George Orwell im gelobten Land: Das Buch Deuteronomium und der Geist kirchlicher Kontrolle," *Kirche und Visitation* (ed. E. W. Zeeden & P. Th. Lang; Stuttgart, 1984), 21–35; idem, "Segregation and Intolerance," *What the Bible Really Says* (ed. M. Smith & R. J. Hoffmann; New York: Prometheus Books, 1993), 115–35.

78. Thus P. Wernle, *The Beginnings of Christianity* (2 vols.; New York: Putnam, 1904), 1:x.

79. Wernle, *Beginnings* 2:258–59, 276–78; H. J. Holtzmann, *Lehrbuch der neutestamentlichen Theologie I* (2nd ed.; Freiburg i. B. & Leipzig, 1911), 540–41.

80. Schüssler Fiorenza, "Ethics," 15, hit on the right word: we are to *"revive* a responsible ethical and political criticism which recognizes the ideological distortions of great works of religion" (my italics).

81. Stendahl, *Meanings*, 4.

82. M. Tindal, *Christianity as Old as the Creation*, reprinted in *History of British Deism* (London: Routledge, 1995), 238.

83. Cf. Barr, *Concept*, 80.

84. Barr, *Concept*, 81, notes that the "generating force" within historical criticism "was the large amount of apparently historical narrative within the Bible… and the very large extent to which Christian doctrine was developed on the basis of these narratives, traditionally treated as historically accurate."

85. For a sample see K. Syreeni, "Separation and Identity," *NTS* 40 (1994): 522–41. For an effort to integrate narrative criticism with the historical approach see now the articles in *Characterization in the Gospels: Reconceiving Narrative Criticism* (ed. D. M. Rhoads & K. Syreeni; Sheffield: Sheffield Academic Press 1999).

86. Contrast F. F. Segovia, "Toward Intercultural Criticism: A Reading Strategy from the Diaspora, " *Reading from this Place, Vol.* 2, 303–30, 303.

87. See my *Das koranische Jesusbild* (Helsinki: Finnische Gesellschaft für Missiologie und Ökumenik, 1971) and *Marcion*, 81–97, 254–58.

88. See my *The Idea of Divine Hardening* (Helsinki: Finnish Exegetical Society, 1972), esp. 8–9; *Marcion*, 98–117, 258–60, esp. 99.

89. *Paul and the Law* (2nd edition; Tübingen: J. C. B. Mohr, 1987).

90. Cf. my article "Comparative Religion, Theology, and New Testament Exegesis," *StudTheol* 52 (1998): 116–29.

91. Schottroff, "Working for Liberation," 190, rightly complains about the treatment of Gnosticism by many older critics (including Bultmann and Braun). Today the situation is quite different, however.

92. Schüssler Fiorenza, "Ethics," 15.

93. I cannot but agree with M. W. Dube, "Savior of the World but not of This World: A Postcolonial Reading of Spatial Construction in John," in *The Postcolonial Bible* (ed. R. S. Sugirtharajah; Sheffield: Sheffield Academic Press, 1998), 118–35, 133, when she "calls for an academic biblical studies that also assesses the impact of biblical texts on modern and contemporary international relations."

94. U. Luz, *Das Evangelium nach Matthäus 1–3* (Zürich: Benziger & Neukirchener Verlag, 1985–97); idem., *Matthew in History: Interpretation, Influence, and Effects* (Minneapolis: Fortress, 1994).

95. R. P. Carroll, *Wolf in the Sheepfold: The Bible as a Problem for Christianity* (London: SPCK, 1991); Lüdemann, *The Unholy*. If I hesitate to include here David Clines's program of hard-hitting ideological criticism, which he also calls a "Bible readers' liberation movement," it is only because he may not consider himself a "historical critic" any more (though he would, in my opinion, certainly qualify as one—one of the more perceptive critics, that is).

96. R. Jewett, *The Captain America Complex: The Dilemma of Zealous Nationalism* (rev. ed.; Santa Fe: Bear, 1984).

97. M. Desjardins, *Peace, Violence and the New Testament* (Sheffield: Sheffield Academic Press, 1997).

98. M. Prior, *Colonialism and the Bible* (Sheffield: Sheffield Academic Press, 1997); idem., *Zionism and the State of Israel* (London: Routledge, 1999), esp. 157–83.

99. Prior, *Colonialism*, 12; cf. 295–96. I should mention that, when in the Lahti conference Prior presented an (invited) paper on "Zionism and the Bible," it evoked fierce reactions from some colleagues in what had been intended to be a scholarly discussion of a topical issue.

100. The bad fruits include anti-Judaism and the troubles caused through centuries by the passages on the unforgivable sin against the Spirit: Luz, *Matthew*, 33.

101. Ibid., 86–87 (my italics).

102. Ibid., 100–101. Actually Luz says that the Bible "does not *want* to function" as a norm etc., but such personification of the book should be avoided.

103. Ibid., 101.

104. Jewett, *Captain America*, 18.

105. Ibid., 146.

106. Ibid., 4 (my italics).

107. Tolbert, "Resistance," 345–46.

108. Thus, M. W. Dube, "Reading for Decolonization (John 4:1-42)," *Semeia* 75 (1996): 37–59, while insisting that "biblical practice must be dedicated to an ethical task of promoting decolonization," will not do this by manipulating the exegesis; on the contrary, she underlines what she regards as "imperial goals, strat-

egies, and values" in John 4 (ibid., 53). Likewise, Dube, "Savior,"
119, sets out to "decolonize Jesus' highly exalted divinity and his
place of origin insofar as they will be shown to express a colonizing
ideology." Cf. Segovia, "Intercultural Criticism," 329: the Bible is
not necessarily an "effective weapon" or "faithful ally" but "a part
of our historical and religious tradition that must be dealt with
and engaged critically." R. C. Bailey, "The Danger of Ignoring
One's Own Cultural Bias in Interpreting the Text," *The Postcolonial
Bible*, 66–90, 79: while the "Eurocentric" interpretations given to
biblical texts are a problem, "there are also passages in the biblical
text itself, which are contrary to our [= Afrocentric interpreters]
experience of God, and we need to confront those with the discontinuity"; cf. ibid., 83. I find myself in full agreement with the whole
of Bailey's article.

109. R. S. Sugirtharajah, "A Postcolonial Exploration of Collu-
sion and Construction in Biblical Interpretation," in *The
Postcolonial Bible*, 91–116, 95–100, criticizes the mobilization of Matthew's missionary commission (Matt 28:19) in commentaries for
Indian students "as a biblical warrant to missionize the natives"
(ibid., 95). But he himself stresses that it was William Carey, the
Baptist missionary pioneer, who "reactivated" this "dormant" text
"as a missionary command for the modern period" in a pamphlet
in 1792. "Since then, this verse has exercised a considerable influence on the institutionalized missionary efforts of the Christian
church" (ibid., 96–97). But why should this be imputed as guilt to
the guild of critical exegetes, many of whom have had a notori-
ously difficult relationship with the church? And whether or not it
was "the emergence of many missionary societies in the eighteenth and nineteenth centuries" that "led exegetes to impose a
missionary-journey structure on the Acts" (ibid., 100–107), exegetes themselves pointed out that customary talk about Paul's
journeys easily engenders a wrong picture: M. Dibelius and W. G.
Kümmel, *Paulus* (Berlin: de Gruyter, 1964), 63; F. Hahn, *Mission in
the New Testament* (London: SCM, 1965), 96 n. 2. On Sugirtharajah's
use of a sentence from G. Strecker's *Die Bergpredigt* to bolster his
claim that the historical-critical methods are colonial see above,
note 31. In the same connection Sugirtharajah castigates
"Orientalist" tendencies in the work of J. Jeremias, *The Parables of
Jesus* (London: SCM, 1963). While Jeremias' statement (made in

view of Luke 16:1) on the "people in the East not knowing any-thing about book-keeping or audit" (ibid., 181), along with other statements of his on the "Orientals," is open to criticism, it is vast ex-aggeration to read it as implying a negative evaluation of "the con-tributions the Chinese, Indians and Egyptians" (!) towards the development of present-day mathematics (so Sugirtharajah, "Afterword," 462). And in any case, as far as I can see, Jeremias' com-ment has not been taken up in commentaries on Luke's gospel.

110. C. Rowland & M. Corner, *Liberating Exegesis* (London: SPCK, 1990), 41, quoting C. Mesters.

111. H. Räisänen, *Beyond New Testament Theology* (London: SCM, 1990), 122–36; idem., "Tradition, Experience, Interpretation. A Dialectical Model for Describing the Development of Religious Thought," *Approaching Religion* I ed. T. Ahlbäck (Abo: The Donner Institute, 1999), 215–26.

112. In this perspective, J. L. Segundo is right in making the provocative suggestion that "we must keep . . . writing gospels": J. L. Segundo, *The Historical Jesus of the Synoptics* (London: Orbis Books, 1985), 7. Cf. *The gospel of Lucas Gavilán* by Vicente Leñero (a Mexican liberation theologian), presented by H. Avalos in *Semeia* 75 (1996): 87–105. Consider also the selective and creative use of the Bible in Negro Spirituals: K. R. Connor, "'Everybody Talking about Heaven Ain't Going There': The Biblical Call for Justice and the Postcolonial Response of the Spirituals," *Semeia* 75 (1996): 107–28; Bailey, "Danger."

113. On the Gentile woman see e.g. J. Perkinson, "A Canaanitic Word in the Logos of Christ; or The Difference the Syro-Phoeni-cian Woman Makes to Jesus," *Semeia* 75 (1996): 61–85; cf. Donaldson, "Postcolonialism," 7.

114. Cf. my chapters on Joseph Smith and Gandhi: *Marcion*, 153–88.

115. D. Seeley, *Deconstructing the New Testament* (Leiden: Brill, 1994), 87–89, argues that there is a sense in which Jesus seems un-necessary in Lukan soteriology, in which salvation is "by generos-ity" (cf. Luke 12:33, 14:12-14, 19:8-9, 10:25); the story of the rich man and Lazarus (Luke 16) reveals that, for Luke, "Moses and the prophets contain everything people need to know." The reason for this is, according to Seeley, Luke's eagerness to affirm "the fun-damental unity of Judaism and Christianity"; Luke, however,

"overdid things, and left the impression that this unity was so complete as to render Jesus expendable." In *Marcion*, 9–12, I point out a similar contradiction between christological exclusivism and a tendency towards others (in this case, Gentiles) in the Areopagus speech (Acts 17). Luke seems to be wrestling with the problem of pluralism and exclusivism (ibid, 200): "Somehow he seems to sense the problematic nature of his own exclusivist standpoint. He is—fortunately—not able simply to brush aside the considerations dictated by universal morality. A kind of incipient universalism does get the opportunity to enter through the back door." Cf. also Perkinson, "A Canaanitic Word," 69: Matt 15:21-28 "can be read as a moment when, in its very genesis, christology offers us a detail that questions its own powers of normativity as discourse. . . . It constitutes a site where the canonical source of christology can be read against itself as a totalizing authority."

116. Cf. Räisänen, *Marcion*, 118–36, 260–68, on the issue whether historical criticism of the Qur'an could be pursued by Muslims.

117 Cf. Segovia, "And They Began," 9: the historical impulse should not be bypassed; the competing modes of discourse are not mutually exclusive. Even Schüssler Fiorenza, "Ethics," 15–17, seems (in my view) to arrive, at the end of her article, at a strategy of distinguishing between the operations of "descriptive-analytic" and "hermeneutic-evaluative" practice.

118. R. S. Sugirtharajah, "Orientalism, Ethnonationalism and Transnationalism: Shifting Identities and Biblical Interpretation," in *Ethnicity and the Bible* (ed. M. Brett; Leiden: Brill, 1996), 419–29, 423 (my italics).

119. Surely a word for that difference could be "the hermeneutical gap"; cf. above, p. 11.

120. R. S. Sugirtharajah, "Texts are Always with You: Christians and their Bibles." *Hindu-Christian Studies Bulletin* 9 (1996): 8–13, 12. Cf. my broadly similar comments on Paul in *Marcion*, 31–32.

Notes to Chapter 2

1. I want to thank Francis Schüssler Fiorenza and Lyn Miller for their critical feedback and corrections.

2. Elisabeth Schüssler Fiorenza, *Rhetoric and Ethic: The Politics*

of Biblical Studies (Minneapolis: Fortress, 1999). It remains to be seen whether this book will receive the same programmatic attention as Räisänen's paper did.

3. See my articles: "Women in Early Christianity: Methodological Considerations," in *Critical History and Biblical Faith in NT Perspectives* (ed. T. J. Ryan; Villanova: CTS Annual Publication, 1979), 30–58; and "For the Sake of Our Salvation: Biblical Interpretation as Theological Task," *in Sin, Salvation and the Spirit* (ed. Daniel Durken; Collegeville: Liturgical Press, 1979), 21–39, although I have changed the nomenclature over the years. Obviously, such a change in naming always also entails a shift in content and accentuation.

4. Fernando F. Segovia, "Cultural Studies and Contemporary Biblical Criticism: Ideological Criticism as a Mode of Discourse," in *Reading from This Place, Vol. 2: Social Location and Biblical Interpretation in Global Perspective* (ed. Fernando F. Segovia and Mary Ann Tolbert; Minneapolis: Fortress, 1995), 1–17. See also his contribution "Biblical Criticism and Postcolonial Studies: Toward a Postcolonial Optic," in *The Postcolonial Bible* (ed. R. S. Sugirtharajah; Sheffield: Sheffield Academic Press, 1998), 49–65.

5. See my *Priester für Gott: Studien zum Herrschafts-und Priestermotiv in der Apokalypse* (NTAbh 7; Münster: Aschendorff, 1972) and *The Book of Revelation: Justice and Judgment* (Minneapolis: Fortress, 1985; 2nd expanded ed., 1998).

6. See my *In Memory of Her: A Feminist Theological Reconstruction of Christian Origins* (New York: Crossroad, 1983; Tenth Anniversary Edition, 1994); *Bread Not Stone: The Challenge of Feminist Biblical Interpretation* (Boston: Beacon Press, 1985; Tenth Anniversary Edition, 1995); *But She Said: Feminist Practices of Biblical Interpretation* (Boston: Beacon Press, 1992); *Jesus. Miriam's Child, Sophia's Prophet: Critical Issues in Feminist Christology* (New York: Continuum, 1994); *Sharing Her Word: Feminist Biblical Interpretation in Context* (Boston: Beacon Press, 1998).

7. Robert Hariman, "Status, Marginality, and Rhetorical Theory," in J. L. Lucaites, C. M. Conduit, and S. Caudill, eds., *Contemporary Rhetorical Theory: A Reader* (New York: The Guilford Press, 1999), 35–51, 42.

8. For a discussion of new directions in historiography see Dominick LaCapra, *Rethinking Intellectual History: Texts, Contexts,*

Language (Ithaca: Cornell University Press, 1983); Georg G. Iggers, *Historiography in the Twentieth Century: From Scientific Objectivity to the Postmodern Challenge* (Hannover: Wesleyan University Press 1997); Keith Jenkins, ed., *The Postmodern History Reader* (New York: Routledge, 1997); Mark Poster, *Cultural History + Postmodernity: Disciplinary Readings and Challenges* (New York: Columbia University Press, 1997). For a discussion of the relationship between historical criticism and theological interpretation see Roy A. Harrisville and Walter Sundberg, *The Bible in Modern Culture: Theology and Historical-Critical Method from Spinoza to Käsemann* (Grand Rapids: Eerdmans, 1995).

9. Heikki Räisänen, "Biblical Critics in the Global Village" [Chapter 1, above], 8.

10. Ibid., 22.

11. Ibid., 21.

12. Ibid., 11.

13. Ibid.

14. Ibid., 13 n. 51.

15. Ibid., 13.

16. Krister Stendahl, "Biblical Theology, Contemporary," in *The Interpreter's Dictionary of the Bible*, 4 vols. (Nashville: Abingdon, 1962), 1:418–32 [reprinted as Appendix 1 in this volume].

17. Krister Stendahl, *Meanings: The Bible as Document and as Guide* (Philadelphia: Fortress, 1984), 1.

18. Krister Stendahl, "Ancient Scripture in the Modern World," in *Scripture in the Jewish and Christian Traditions: Antiquity, Interpretation, Relevance* (ed. Frederick Greenspahn; Nashville: Abingdon, 1982), 201–14, 204.

19. The literature is extensive. See for instance Walter H. Capps, *The New Religious Right: Piety, Patriotism and Politics* (Columbia: University of South Carolina Press, 1990); Lawrence Grossberg, *We Gotta Get Out of This Place: Popular Conservatism and Postmodern Culture* (New York: Routledge, 1992); Sara Diamond, *Spiritual Warfare: the Politics of the Christian Right* (Boston; South End Press, 1989); James Hunter, *Culture Wars: The Struggle to Define America* (New York: Basic Books, 1991); Michael Barkun, *Religion and the Racist Right: The Origins of the Christian Identity Movement* (Chapel Hill: University of North Carolina Press, 1994); David

Rose, ed., *The Emergence of David Duke and the Politics of Race,* (Chapel Hill: University of North Carolina Press, 1992).

20. Because my work is engaged in contemporary hermeneutical questions rather than just in antiquarian historical studies, it was made a condition of my appointment at Harvard Divinity School (1988!) that my affiliation and teaching be split between the areas of historical-critical NT Studies and "Religion and Society."

21. I have resorted to writing wo/men in such a fragmented way in order to indicate the ambiguity and the inclusivity of the term. What wo/men means depends on its racial, class, and ethnic-cultural inflection. In addition, wo/man includes man and s/he includes he. Hence, I use wo/men in the same sense as the term "human" is generally used, a term which is typed as elite male. See my book *Sharing Her Word: The Context of Biblical Interpretation* (Boston: Beacon Press, 1998).

22. R. S. Sugirtharajah, "The Margin as a Site of Creative Revisioning," in *Voices from the Margin: Interpreting the Bible in the Third World* (ed. R. S. Sugirtharajah; rev. ed.; Maryknoll: Orbis, 1995), 1–8.

23. Wayne A. Meeks, *The Origins of Christian Morality: The First Two Centuries* (New Haven: Yale University Press, 1993), 4.

24. For such an argument see Gerd Theissen, "Methodenkonkurrenz und hermeneutischer Konflikt: Pluralismus in Exegese und Lektüre der Bibel," in *Pluralismus und Identität* (ed. Joachim Mehlhausen; Gütersloh: Chr. Kaiser Gütersloher Verlagshaus, 1995), 127–40.

Notes to Chapter 3

1. John Colenso, *St. Paul's Epistle to the Romans, Newly Translated and Examined from a Missionary Point of View* (Cambridge: Macmillan, 1861); see Jonathan A. Draper, "Hermeneutical Dram on the Colonial Stage: Liminal Space and Creativity in Colenso's Commentary on Romans," *Journal of Theology for Southern Africa* 103 (March 1999): 13–32.

2. Georg Strecker, *The Sermon on the Mount: An Exegetical Commentary* (Nashville: Abingdon, 1988), 9. I owe this point to Daniel Patte.

3. S. Thoburn, *Old Testament Introduction* (The Christian Students' Library 24; Madras: The Christian Literature Society, 1961), 34.

4. A. Hanson, *Jonah and Daniel: Introduction and Commentary* (The Christian Students' Library 9; Madras: The Christian Literature Society, 1961), 34.

5. Most of the materials in the preceding paragraphs are based on S. N. Balagangadhara's work. I have not only used freely his concepts but also some of his phrases and vocabularies. See his *'The Heathen in His Blindness . . . ': Asia, the West and the Dynamic of Religion* (Leiden: Brill, 1994), 408–13.

6. Cited in W. Neil, "The Criticism and Theological Use of the Bible, 1700–1950," in *The Cambridge History of the Bible: The West from the Reformation to the Present Day* (ed. S. L. Greenslade; Cambridge: Cambridge University Press, 1963), 286.

7. Edward W. Said, *Representations of the Intellectual* (London: Vintage, 1994), 89.

8. David Spurr, *The Rhetoric of the Empire: Colonial Discourse in Journalism, Travel Writing* (Durham: Duke University Press, 1993), 92–93.

Notes to Chapter 4

1. The impact of the biblical tradition(s) and their interpretations on the society at large is worth special attention. For here their power is (a) deeply bedded in cultural patterns and habits of thought and (b) hence often hidden, and (c) there is no recourse to theological critique and re-interpretations. Long after the theological renewal by, for example, feminist hermeneutics have changed much of the churches' thinking, the old ways will play into much of Western society. There will also be "the fundamentalism of the non-believers" by which literal and biblicistic Christianity is hailed as the true and only one and other interpretations are deemed just embarrassed manipulations.

2. In my essay on "Biblical Theology" included in this volume, I referred explicitly to how I thought the distinction between what it "meant" and what it might "mean" is of special importance for "theology on the mission field and in the young churches," p. 104.

3. *Marcion, Muhammad and the Mahatma: Exegetical Perspectives on the Encounter of Cultures and Faiths* (London: SCM, 1997).

4. *Journal of Ecumenical Studies* 22 (1985): 242–60. Cf. his *Sinai and Zion: An Entry into the Jewish Bible* (Minneapolis: Fortress, 1985), 109: "The polemical misrepresentation of Canaanite and other 'pagan' religion in the Hebrew Bible parallels the polemical misrepresentation of Pharisaism (or Judaism) in the New Testament. My impression is that American Christian Scholars are now more willing to concede the latter than Jewish scholars are to concede the former." Räisänen holds up the European flank.

5. For that same reason I claimed that "meaning" is always a meaning to somebody—the author, the hearer, the readers in full diachronic and synchronic diversity. There is no disembodied "meaning" in the text which the proper exegetical method can detect. The question must be: meaning to whom? And if that "who" be God, let the interpreter say so.

6. Thus I agree with James Barr in his critique of that point in his most fair discussion of my 1962 article in *The Interpreter's Dictionary of the Bible*. I have more difficulty grasping his argument about how "Biblical theology is not looking for what it *meant*, but for *what it was*"; see James Barr, *The Concept of Biblical Theology* (1999), esp. 202–204 [reprinted as Appendix 3 in this volume; see p. 143]. Is my difficulty with that line of thinking my insistence that any reference to what it meant/means requires an explicit "to whom?"

7. See, for example, *Marcion*, 199–200.

8. I am, of course, aware of the anachronism in calling Paul a "Christian" as the word came to be used. For him Gentiles who came to faith in Jesus Christ were thereby brought to the God of Abraham, Isaac and Jacob. There was no new "religion."

9. In *Marcion*, 200, in the section on reading against the grain, Räisänen says: "Indeed, if I am on the right track in my reading of Romans 9–11, it is Paul's struggle, his wrestling with his tradition in the light of new experiences, that might be seen as a model for us, as his weightiest contribution to contemporary struggles." I think we are more in agreement in our reading of Rom 11:11–36 than appears in Räisänen's grand article "Romans 9–11 and the "History of Early Christian Religion" in T. Fornberg et al. eds, *Texts and Contexts: Essays in Honor of Lars Hartman* (Scandinavian Uni-

versity Press). I feel that Räisänen, like Alan Segal and many others, read me as if I would have Paul teach "two ways of salvation," one for Jews and one for Gentiles. That looks to me as a traffic plan. I rather see Paul as reminding his Gentile converts that God's ways are mysterious and beyond self-serving ideas.

On these matters I have come to change my views from the ones I held in the 1960s when I wrote the essay on "Biblical Theology" included in the volume [as Appendix 1]. See now the chapter "Missiological Reflections of a Former Zealot: Romans 9–11" in my *Final Account: Paul's Letter to the Romans* (Minneapolis: Fortress, 1995).

10. See my articles "Qumran and Supersessionism—and The Road Not Taken," *The Princeton Seminary Bulletin* 19 (1998): 134–42, and "From God's Perspective We Are All Minorities," *Journal of Religious Pluralism* 2 (1993): 1–13.

Notes to Appendix 2

1. Frank C. Porter, "The Bearing of Historical Studies on the Religious Use of the Bible," *HTR* 2 (1909): 276.

2. Amos N. Wilder articulated this literary-aesthetic paradigm as rhetorical. See his SBL presidential address, "Scholars, Theologians, and Ancient Rhetoric," *JBL* 75 (1956):1-11 and his book *Early Christian Rhetoric: The Language of the Gospel* (Cambridge: Harvard University Press, 1971)

3. Richard Harvey Brown, *Society as Text: Essays on Rhetoric, Reason, and Reality* (Chicago: University of Chicago Press, 1987) 85. See also, e.g., J. Nelson, A. Megills, and D. McCloskey, eds., *The Rhetoric of the Human Sciences: Language and Argument in Scholarship and Public Affairs* (Madison: University of Wisconsin Press, 1987); Hayden White, *Tropics of Discourse: Essays in Cultural Criticism* (Baltimore: Johns Hopkins University Press, 1978); Ricca Edmondsen, *Rhetoric in Sociology* (New York: Cambridge University Press, 1985); John S. Nelson, "Political Theory as Political Rhetoric," in *What Should Political Theory Be Now?* (ed. J. S. Nelson; Albany: State University of New York Press, 1983), 169–240.

4. See my article "Rhetorical Situation and Historical Reconstruction in I Corinthians," *NTS* 33 (1987): 386–403, and Wilhelm

Wuellner, "Where is Rhetorical Criticism Taking Us?" *CBQ* 49 (1987): 448–63 for further literature.

5. For bringing together the insights of this paper I have found especially helpful the works of feminist literary and cultural criticism. See, e.g., S. Benhabib and D. Cornwell, eds., *Feminism as Critique* (Minneapolis: University of Minnesota Press, 1987); Gayatri Chakravorty Spivak, *In Other Worlds: Essays in Cultural Politics* (New York: Methuen, 1987); Theresa de Laurentis, ed., *Feminist Studies/Critical Studies* (Bloomington: University of Indiana Press, 1986); E. A. Flynn and P. P. Schweickart, eds., *Gender and Reading: Essays on Reader, Texts, and Contexts* (Baltimore, MD: Johns Hopkins University Press, 1986); G. Greene and C. Kaplan, eds., *Making a Difference: Feminist Literary Criticism* (New York: Methuen, 1983); Elizabeth A. Meese, *Crossing the Double Cross: The Practice of Feminist Criticism* (Chapel Hill: University of North Carolina Press, 1986); J. Newton and D. Rosenfelt, eds., *Feminist Criticism and Social Change* (New York: Methuen, 1985); M. Pryse and Hortense J. Spillers, eds., *Conjuring: Black Women, Fiction and Literary Tradition* (Bloomington: University of Indiana Press, 1985); Chris Weedon, *Feminist Practice and Poststructuralist Theory* (London: Blackwell, 1987).

6. J. Hillis Miller, "Presidential Address 1986. The Triumph of Theory, the Resistance to Reading, and the Question of the Material Base," *PMLA* 102 (1987): 284.

7. Michael Walzer characterizes the "connected critic" as follows: "Amos prophecy is social criticism because it challenges the leaders, the conventions, the ritual practices of a particular society and because it does so in the name of values shared and recognized in that same society" (*Interpretation and Social Criticism* [Cambridge: Harvard University Press, 1987], 89)

8. Virginia Woolf, *Three Guineas* (New York: Harcourt, Brace, Jovanovich, 1966), 61.

9. For the following information, see Dorothy C. Bass, "Women's Studies and Biblical Studies: An Historical Perspective," *JSOT* 22 (1982): 6–12; Ernest W. Saunders, *Searching the Scriptures: A History of the Society of Biblical Literature, 1880–1980* (Chico, Calif.: Scholars Press, 1982), 70, 83f.; and Carolyn De Swarte Gifford, "American Women and the Bible: The Nature of Women as A Hermeneutical Issue," in *Feminist Perspectives on Biblical Scholar-*

ship (ed. A. Yarbro Collins; Chico, Calif.: Scholars Press, 1985), 11–33.

10. To my knowledge only one Afro-American and one Asian -American woman have yet received a doctorate in biblical studies.

11. Bass, "Women's Studies," 10–11.

12. Barbara Brown Zikmund, "Biblical Arguments and Women's Place in the Church," in *The Bible And Social Reform* (ed. E. R. Sandeen; Philadelphia: Fortress, 1982), 85–104; For Jarena Lee, see William L. Andrews, ed., *Sisters of the Spirit: Three Black Women's Autobiographies of the Nineteenth Century* (Bloomington: Indiana University Press, 1986).

13. Elizabeth Cady Stanton, ed., *The Original Feminist Attack on the Bible: The Woman's Bible* (1895, 1898; facsimile ed., New York: Arno, 1974), 1.9; see also Elaine C. Huber, "They Weren't Prepared to Hear: A Closer Look at the Woman's Bible," *ANQ* 16 (1976): 271–76, and Anne McGrew Bennett et al., "The Woman's Bible: Review and Perspectives," in *Women and Religion: 1973 Proceedings* (Tallahassee: AAR, 1973), 39–78.

14. Lee Anna Starr, *The Bible Status of Women* (New York: Fleming Revell, 1926); Katherine C. Bushnell, *God's Word to Women: One Hundred Bible Studies on Woman's Place in the Divine Economy* (1923; reissued by Ray Munson, North Collins, NY).

15. Margaret Brackenbury Crook, *Women and Religion* (Boston: Beacon Press, 1964); see also Elsie Thomas Culver, *Women in the World of Religion* (Garden City, N.Y.: Doubleday, 1967).

16. Schüssler Fiorenza, *In Memory of Her: A Feminist Theological Reconstruction of Christian Origins* (New York: Crossroad, 1983); Schüssler Fiorenza, *Bread Not Stone: The Challenge of Feminist Biblical Interpretation* (Boston: Beacon Press, 1985).

17. See Calvin O. Schrag, *Communicative Praxis and the Space of Subjectivity* (Bloomington: Indiana University Press, 1986), 179–214.

18. I want to thank Ann Millin, Episcopal Divinity School, for checking SBL presidential addresses for references to and reflections of their political contexts as well as Margaret Hutaff, Harvard Divinity School, for proofreading the manuscript. I am also indebted to Francis Schüssler Fiorenza for his critical reading of several drafts of this essay.

19. Robert W. Funk, "The Watershed of The American Biblical Tradition: The Chicago School, First Phase, 1892–1920," *JBL* 95 (1976): 7.

20. Letter to Erich Förster, pastor and professor in Frankfurt, as quoted by Walter Schmithals, *An Introduction to the Theology of Rudolf Bultmann* (Minneapolis: Augsburg, 1968), 9–10; See also Dorothe Soelle, "Rudolf Bultmann und die Politische Theologie," in *Rudolf Bultmann: 100 Jahre* (ed. H. Thyen; Oldenburger Vorträge; Oldenburg: H. Holzberg, 1985), 69ff.; and Dieter Georgi, "Rudolf Bultmann's Theology of the New Testament Revisited," in *Bultmann Retrospect and Prospect: The Centenary Symposium at Wellesley* (ed. E. C. Hobbs; HTS 35; Philadelphia: Fortress, 1985), 82ff.

21. Morton S. Enslin, "The Future of Biblical Studies," *JBL* 65 (1946): 1–12; Already Julian Morgenstern had argued "that in Germany biblical science is doomed." Since in Europe Biblical Studies are in decline, North America, i.e., the U.S. and Canada "must become the major center of biblical research" ("The Society of Biblical Literature and Exegesis," *JBL* 61 [1942]: 4–5).

22. George G. Iggers, *The German Conception of History: The National Tradition of Historical Thought from Herder to the Present* (rev. ed.; Middletown, Conn.: Wesleyan University Press, 1983) 64.

23. Robert A. Oden, Jr., "Hermeneutics and Historiography: Germany and America," in SBL 1980 *Seminar Papers* (ed. P. J. Achtemeier; Chico, Calif.: Scholars Press, 1980), 135–57.

24. James A. Montgomery, "Present Tasks of American Biblical Scholarship," *JBL* 38 (1919): 2.

25. Henry J. Cadbury, "Motives of Biblical Scholarship," *JBL* 56 (1937): 1–16.

26. Leroy Waterman, "Biblical Studies in a New Setting," *JBL* 66 (1947): 5.

27. Ibid.

28. David Tracy, *Plurality and Ambiguity: Hermeneutics, Religion, and Hope* (New York: Harper & Row, 1987), 31.

29. See the discussion of scientific theory choice by Linda Alcoff, "Justifying Feminist Social Science," *Hypatia* 2 (1987): 107–27.

30. Maurice Mandelbaum, *The Anatomy of Historical Knowledge* (Baltimore: Johns Hopkins University Press, 1977), 150.

31. Krister Stendahl, "The Bible as a Classic and the Bible as Holy Scripture," *JBL* 103 (1984): 10.

32. See Wayne C. Booth, "Freedom of Interpretation: Bakhtin and the Challenge of Feminist Criticism," in *The Politics of Interpretation* (ed. J. T. Mitchell; Chicago: University of Chicago Press, 1983), 51–82.

33. See Francis Schüssler Fiorenza, "Theory and Practice: Theological Education as a Reconstructive, Hermeneutical and Practical Task," *Theological Education* 23 (1987): 113–41.

34. See also Ronald F. Thiemann, "Toward an American Public Theology: Religion in a Pluralistic Theology," *Harvard Divinity Bulletin* 18/1 (1987): 3–6, 10.

Notes to Appendix 3

1. *The Interpreter's Dictionary of the Bible*, 4 vols. (New York and Nashville: Abingdon, 1962), 1:418–32 [reprinted as Appendix 1 in this volume].

2. Also now Francis Watson; see pp. 141–43 below.

3. See James D. Smart, *The Past, Present and Future of Biblical Theology* (Philadelphia: Westminster, 1979), 41–3; quotation 43.

4. Brevard S. Childs, "Interpretation in Faith: The Theological Responsibility of an Old Testament Commentary," *Interpretation* 18 (1964): 432–49; quoted by Stendahl, "Method in the Study of Biblical Theology," in *The Bible in Modern Scholarship* (ed. J. P. Hyatt; Nashville: Abingdon, 1965), 203 n. 13. On Stendahl's views see further below.

5. Contrast Ben C. Ollenburger, who, in his "What Krister Stendahl 'meant'—A Normative Critique of 'Descriptive Biblical Theology'," *HBT* 8 (1986): 61–98, surely the best modern discussion of the matter, disagrees with Stendahl on this matter but examines the arguments in detail, entirely avoids any negative criticism of Stendahl, and writes that "his contributions to biblical scholarship have been major and exemplary" (63).

6. In this, however, I should add that there has probably been a change between the time when Stendahl wrote—doubtless in the late 1950s, since his article was published in 1962—and the present time of writing. With the rise of postmodernism, cynicism towards "objectivity" has escalated enormously since that time.

7. Ollenburger, 61. Cf. perhaps the judgment of Childs, *Biblical Theology in Crisis* (Philadelphia: Westminster Press, 1970), 79, that "Stendahl's article received such a ready response because he advocated what was, in fact, already happening. Certainly *The Interpreter's Bible* dramatically illustrated in its format the austere separation of descriptive exegesis and theology." I very much doubt, however, whether Stendahl considered the format of *The Interpreter's Bible* to represent what he intended.

8. Walter Brueggemann, *Old Testament Theology: Essays on Structure, Themes, and Text* (ed. Patrick D. Miller; Minneapolis: Fortress, 1992), 111. Note similarly the opinion of Leo G. Perdue, *The Collapse of History: Reconstructing Old Testament Theology* (Minneapolis: Fortress, 1994), 9, who notes "an increasing number of biblical theologians rejecting the descriptive approach."

9. Thus Smart held up for derision, marked by his exclamation mark, the idea, supposed by him to follow from Stendahl's thinking, that "All that is needed is an adequate historical methodology. The agnostic can tell us the meaning of what the first Christians testified concerning the cross and the resurrection of Jesus!"—so his *Past, Present and Future of Biblical Theology*, 42.

10. Th. C. Vriezen, *An Outline of Old Testament Theology* (2nd ed.; Oxford: Blackwell, 1970; 1st ed., 1958; 1st Dutch ed., 1949; much revised in the 3rd Dutch ed., 1966).

11. Childs, "Interpretation in Faith," 432–49.

12. Stendahl, "Method in the Study of Biblical Theology," 203 n. 13. Stendahl's note contains further useful arguments. On his views see further below.

13. For Frank Kermode's discussion of Childs' proposal and of my criticisms of it, see his "Canons" [a review of J. Barr, *Holy Scriptures: Canon, Authority, Criticism* and E. Leach and D. A. Aycock, *Structuralist Interpretation of Biblical Myth*] in *London Review of Books* (2–15 February 1984): 3–4.

14. Childs, *Old Testament Theology in a Canonical Context* (London: SCM, 1985), 12.

15. Childs, *Biblical Theology of the Old and New Testaments* (London: SCM, 1992), 93f.

16. In his recent article "Old Testament Theology" in James L. Mays, David L. Petersen, and Kent H. Richards, eds., *Old Testament Interpretation: Past, Present, and Future* (Nashville: Abingdon, 1995),

293–301, Childs says that Eichrodt made an "appeal to objectivity" (295), but I do not think that this is true. He went no farther than asserting the principles as I have stated above.

17. As set forth in his article "Biblical Theology, Contemporary," see note 1 above.

18. On this see Krister Stendahl, *The Bible and the Role of Women: A Case Study in Hermeneutics* (Philadelphia: Fortress, 1966).

19. See James Barr, *The Garden of Eden and the Hope of Immortality* (London: SCM, 1992), esp. 2, 52f., 94–99.

20. Ibid.

21. See Stendahl, "The Apostle Paul and the Introspective Conscience of the West," *HTR* 56 (1963): 199–215. Note an interesting retort against Stendahl by Peter Stuhlmacher, *Biblische Theologie des Neuen Testaments* I (Göttingen: Vandenhoeck & Ruprecht, 1992), 239ff., who takes Stendahl's ideas (and those of some others, e.g. A. F. Segal, E. P. Sanders, H. Räisänen, J. D. G. Dunn) as "attacks" on justification by faith and seeks to vindicate what he himself calls the "German" view of it. Cf. also Childs, *Biblical Theology*, 245, who classifies Stendahl's view, along with those of A. Schweitzer and E. P. Sanders, as "a popular liberal construal of Paul." I cannot see how Stendahl's view on this subject, whether right or wrong, can be correctly classified as "liberal"; on the contrary, I have noticed the warm welcome it has received from many whose theological judgment would count as distinctly "conservative." Francis Watson mentions as part of this "de-Lutheranization" of Paul such distinctly non-liberal scholars as Markus Barth, J. D. G. Dunn, and N. T. Wright: see his *Paul, Judaism and the Gentiles* (Cambridge: Cambridge University Press, 1986), 18, and Chapters 1 and 10 in general.

22. Heikki Räisänen, *Beyond New Testament Theology* (London: SCM, 1990), 112. The example is germane, because Stendahl mentions Schweitzer quite a lot in his article on "Biblical Theology," *IDB* 1:418–19 [reprinted as Appendix 1 in this volume; see pp. 69–71 above].

23. Thus Childs, *Biblical Theology in Crisis*, observes that: "One often gained the impression that what distinguished Biblical Theology from the disciplined study of the Old and New Testaments was a homiletical topping" (93). This was, as he put it, "one of the soft spots" of the movement. On the other hand, in the same pages

he emphasizes the involvement in a present task. "If Biblical studies are to remain vibrant for theology, they must benefit from active confrontation with the new questions of the age, and not be allowed to slip back into a state of scholarly antiquarianism" (ibid., 94f.). Biblical theology, Childs goes on to argue, must be revived and continued because "Christian pastors" need it. They need to have a "theological synthesis" of their own (95). But this does not answer the key question. It does not explain why their theological synthesis must consist of *biblical* theology: why should it not consist of dogmatic theology?

24. Cf. Perdue, *The Collapse of History*, 9, who writes: "The descriptive approach also does not attempt to engage present culture, leaving that task to those contemporary theologians (e.g., Paul Tillich) who see modern culture as an important consideration in theological discourse." Stendahl's position is that there are two distinct *operations*, not that the second stage should or must be left to some other group of persons. He himself, as illustrated above, very much "engaged present culture."

25. Matitiahu Tsevat, "Theologie des Alten Testaments—eine jüdische Sicht," in *Mitte der Schrift? Ein jüdische-christliches Gespräch* (ed. Martin Klopfenstein; Bern: Peter Lang, 1987), 329–41, esp. 333f. He describes Stendahl's formulation as short and clear, but then goes on to explain it in the terms as stated above, yet with the qualification that it does not appear so in Stendahl's version (*wiewohl anscheinend nicht in der Fassung Stendahls*). Tsevat goes on to plead that there should be no more exegesis of the Old Testament "for our times" (335).

26. Friedrich Mildenberger, "Biblische Theologie versus Dogmatik?" *JBTh* 6 (1991): 269–81, esp. 273f. For further discussion of Mildenberger's general position see my *The Concept of Biblical Theology*, Chapter 29.

27. Francis Watson, *Text, Church and World* (Edinburgh: T&T Clark, 1994), 30–33. There is a further note to the same effect in his later *Text and Truth: Redefining Biblical Theology* (Edinburgh: T&T Clark, and Grand Rapids: Eerdmans, 1997), 28 n. 3.

28. See my article "Allegory and Historicism," *JSOT* 69 (1996): 105–20.

29. Cf. the views of John Barton as cited in *The Concept of Biblical Theology*, Chapter 8.

30. See my *Old and New in Interpretation* (London: SCM, and New York: Harper & Row, 1966), 176f., 185–89.

31. See Childs, *Introduction to the Old Testament as Scripture* (London: SCM, 1979), 16; Childs, *Exodus* (Old Testament Library; London: SCM, and Philadelphia: Westminster, 1974), xiii. For an earlier discussion of these examples see my *Holy Scripture: Canon, Authority, Criticism* (Oxford: Clarendon Press, and Philadelphia: Westminster Press, 1983), 151ff.

32. Childs, *Old Testament Theology in a Canonical Context*, 12, cf. again on 14. Francis Watson displays a ludicrous misunderstanding of Childs' thinking when he suggests that this usage on Childs' part is "the standard critical appeal to the "time-conditioned" character of this or that feature of the New Testament texts as a way of excluding it from serious theological and hermeneutical consideration" (*Text and Truth*, 223 n. 41). The argument—though there may indeed be questions about its validity at this particular point—is repeatedly used as an anti-historical-critical one; and who will believe that Childs is seeking to exclude the texts from serious theological and hermeneutical consideration?

33. This is confirmed by the judgment of A. H. J. Gunneweg; see *The Concept of Biblical Theology*, Chapter 26.